PRAYING GOD'S WILL

for
My Pastor

LEE ROBERTS

OLIVER
NELSON

THOMAS NELSON PUBLISHERS
Nashville

To pastors, who have been called with a holy calling, not according to their works, but according to God's own purpose and grace, which was given to them in Christ Jesus before time began.

From 2 Timothy 1:9

Published in Nashville, Tennessee, by Oliver-Nelson Books, a division of Thomas Nelson, Inc., Publishers, and distributed in Canada by Word Communications, Ltd., Richmond, British Columbia.

The Bible version used in this publication is THE NEW KING JAMES VERSION. Copyright © 1979, 1980, 1982, Thomas Nelson, Inc., Publishers. Verses have been modified to fit the prayer format.

Printed in the United States of America.

Library of Congress Cataloging-in-Publication Data

Roberts, Lee, 1941–
    Praying God's will for my pastor / Lee Roberts.
      p.   cm.
    ISBN 0-8407-9250-6 (pbk.)
    1. Prayers for pastors.   I. Title.
BV283.C47R6   1994
242′.8—dc20
                                       93-35673
                                         CIP

1 2 3 4 5 6 — 99 98 97 96 95 94

Contents

About Your Pastor

Your pastor is Bible teacher, personal counselor, business administrator, spiritual leader, officiant at special services, representative to the community, public speaker, preacher—and more.

Your pastor is responsible for bringing God's truth to the people in his pastoral charge and for leading these same people to an understanding of God's love and into an intimate spiritual relationship with Him.

At the same time, however, your pastor's time is beset with pleas to help minimize anguish when marriage partners are betrayed, youngsters are unruly, teenagers are wayward, parents are struggling, singles are lonely, committee members are quarrelsome, families are grieving, building repairs are needed, church school supplies are lacking, facilities are inadequate, and budgets are pinched.

Your pastor works longer hours than most members of his congregation, and he rarely gets a weekend off. He *needs* your prayers to keep going.

The purpose of this book is straightforward: to provide you with an organized way to pray God's perfect will for your pastor. Page after page of prayers have been taken directly from Scripture to help you articulate your pastor's need for guidance and protection for knowing and fulfilling God's will.

Pray for your pastor. Daily.

1

ANGER

Heavenly Father, I pray to You today on behalf of my pastor and in the name of Jesus, Your Son and my Lord and Savior. Like all of us, my pastor sometimes faces situations that can bring about frustration and in some cases even anger. I ask You to hear my prayers which are Your very words from Scripture and to honor these prayers for my pastor. In Jesus' name I pray. Amen.

God, in accordance
with Your word . . .

I pray that my pastor will be swift to hear,
slow to speak, slow to wrath; for his wrath
does not produce the righteousness of God.

JAMES 1:20

———— † ————

I pray that the discretion of my pastor makes
him slow to anger, and it is to his glory to
overlook a transgression.

PROVERBS 19:11

I pray that my pastor will commit his way
to You, LORD, and trust also in You, and You
shall bring it to pass. You shall bring forth
his righteousness as the light, and his justice
as the noonday. I pray that he will rest in
You, LORD, and wait patiently for You. I pray
that he does not fret because of him who
prospers in his way, or because of the person
who brings wicked schemes to pass. I pray
that he will cease from anger, and forsake
wrath; that he does not fret—it only causes
harm.

PSALM 37:5–8

———— † ————

I pray that my pastor will not hasten in his
spirit to be angry, for anger rests in the
bosom of fools.

ECCLESIASTES 7:9

———— † ————

I pray that my pastor understands that a fool
vents all his feelings, but a wise man holds
them back.

PROVERBS 29:11

I pray that my pastor will let all bitterness, wrath, anger, clamor, and evil speaking be put away from him, with all malice. I pray also that he will be kind to others, tenderhearted, forgiving others, just as God in Christ forgave him.

EPHESIANS 4:31–32

---

†

I pray that my pastor knows that if he is slow to anger, he is better than the mighty, and if he rules his spirit, he is better than he who takes a city.

PROVERBS 16:32

---

†

I pray that my pastor realizes that a person who is quick-tempered acts foolishly.

PROVERBS 14:17

---

†

I pray that if my pastor is angry, he will not sin. That he does not let the sun go down on his wrath.

EPHESIANS 4:26

I pray that my pastor will make no friendship with an angry person, and with a furious person he will not go, lest he learn their ways and set a snare for his soul.

PROVERBS 22:24–25

———— † ————

I pray that my pastor always remembers that a soft answer turns away wrath, but a harsh word stirs up anger.

PROVERBS 15:1

2
ATTITUDE

Lord Jesus, my pastor has to face so many problems each day that are not of his own doing. He regularly has to deal with illness, death, marital problems and problems within our church. Today I want to pray Your word over him that he may maintain a proper attitude while he helps us deal with our problems. Thank You for giving me Your words to pray for my pastor. In Your name I pray. Amen.

God, in accordance with Your word . . .

I pray that my pastor knows that he can do all things through Christ who strengthens him.

PHILIPPIANS 4:13

———————— † ————————

I pray that my pastor will not sorrow, for the joy of the LORD is his strength.

NEHEMIAH 8:10

I pray that my pastor will remember whatever things are true, whatever things are noble, whatever things are just, whatever things are pure, whatever things are lovely, whatever things are of good report, if there is any virtue and if there is anything praiseworthy—that he will meditate on these things.

PHILIPPIANS 4:8

———— † ————

I pray that my pastor will remember that this is the day which the LORD has made and that he will rejoice and be glad in it.

PSALM 118:24

———— † ————

I pray that my pastor understands what Jesus meant when He said, "My grace is sufficient for you, for My strength is made perfect in weakness."

2 CORINTHIANS 12:9

I pray that my pastor realizes that in all these things he is more than a conqueror through You who loved him.

ROMANS 8:37

---- † ----

I pray that my pastor will always love You, the Lord his God, with all his heart, with all his soul, with all his mind, and with all his strength and that he will love his neighbor as himself.

MARK 12:30–31

---- † ----

I pray that whatever my pastor does, he does it heartily, as to You, Lord, and not to men.

COLOSSIANS 3:23

3

CONDEMNED

Lord God, I ask You to keep in my pastor's mind at all times that there is no condemnation for those who are in Christ Jesus. Should others ever attempt to unfairly criticize or condemn my pastor I ask you to keep him in your embrace and to lift him, through Christ Jesus, above whatever that situation might be. Thank You, in Jesus' name. Amen.

God, in accordance
with Your word . . .

I pray that my pastor will draw near with a true heart in full assurance of faith, having his heart sprinkled from an evil conscience and his body washed with pure water.

HEBREWS 10:22

——————— † ———————

I pray that as far as the east is from the west, so far have You removed my pastor's transgressions from him.

PSALM 103:12

I pray that my pastor always remembers that You, the LORD his God, are gracious and merciful, and will not turn Your face from him if he returns to You.

2 CHRONICLES 30:9

————— † —————

I pray that my pastor knows that it was You, God, who said that, "I, even I, am He who blots out your transgressions for My own sake."

ISAIAH 43:25

————— † —————

I pray that You did not send Your Son into the world to condemn my pastor, but that my pastor through Him might be saved. He who believes in Him is not condemned.

JOHN 3:17–18

————— † —————

I pray that if my pastor is in You, Christ, he is a new creation; old things have passed away; behold, all things have become new.

2 CORINTHIANS 5:17

I pray that my pastor, who hears Your word, Jesus, and believes in Him who sent You, has everlasting life, and shall not come into judgment, but has passed from death into life.

JOHN 5:24

---------- † ----------

I pray that You, God, will be merciful to my pastor's unrighteousness, and to his sins and to his lawless deeds and that You will remember them no more.

HEBREWS 8:12

---------- † ----------

I pray that my pastor will forsake any wicked ways and any unrighteous thoughts. Let him return to You, LORD, and You will have mercy on him and abundantly pardon him.

ISAIAH 55:7

---------- † ----------

I pray that You forgive my pastor's iniquity, and his sin You will remember no more.

JEREMIAH 31:34

I pray that my pastor will acknowledge his sin to You, God, and his iniquity he will not hide. That he will confess his transgressions to You so You can forgive the iniquity of his sins.

PSALM 32:5

———— † ————

I pray that if my pastor will confess his sins, You, God, are faithful and just to forgive his sins and to cleanse him from all unrighteousness.

1 JOHN 1:9

———— † ————

I pray that my pastor has overcome Satan by the blood of the Lamb and by the word of his testimony.

REVELATION 12:11

———— † ————

I pray that my pastor remembers that Jesus Himself said, "Neither do I condemn you; go and sin no more."

JOHN 8:11

I pray that my pastor is blessed, whose transgression is forgiven, whose sin is covered.

PSALM 32:1

———— † ————

I pray that there is therefore now no condemnation to my pastor who is in Christ Jesus, who does not walk according to the flesh, but according to the Spirit. For the law of the Spirit of life in Christ Jesus has made him free from the law of sin and death.

ROMANS 8:1–2

4

CONFIDENCE

Lord Jesus, every pastor needs to face every day with confidence. Today I ask you to instill in my pastor the confidence that only You can give. Help him to know that he really can do all things through Jesus who gives him strength. Help him to trust You completely and to know that You will never fail him. In Your name I offer these powerful prayers for my pastor. Amen.

God, in accordance with Your word . . .

I pray that when my pastor passes through the waters, You will be with him; and through the rivers, they shall not overflow him. When he walks through the fire, he shall not be burned, nor shall the flame scorch him. For You are the Lord his God.

ISAIAH 43:2–3

I pray that my pastor always remembers that it is You who justify.

ROMANS 8:33

———— † ————

I pray that this is the confidence that my pastor has in You, Jesus, that if he asks anything according to Your will, You hear him. And if he knows that You hear him, whatever he asks, he knows that he has the petitions that he asked of You.

1 JOHN 5:14–15

———— † ————

I pray that when my pastor faces an obstacle he always remembers that God has said that it is "Not by might nor by power, but by My Spirit."

ZECHARIAH 4:6

———— † ————

I pray that whatever my pastor asks in Jesus' name, You will do it.

JOHN 14:14

I pray that You, the LORD God, are my pastor's strength.

HABAKKUK 3:19

———— † ————

I pray that my pastor will not cast away his confidence, which has great reward. For he has need of endurance, so that after he has done Your will, God, he may receive the promise.

HEBREWS 10:35–36

———— † ————

I pray that my pastor will be confident of this very thing, that You who have begun a good work in him will complete it until the day of Jesus Christ.

PHILIPPIANS 1:6

———— † ————

I pray that my pastor can do all things through You who strengthen him.

PHILIPPIANS 4:13

I pray that my pastor may boldly say: "The Lord is my helper; I will not fear. What can man do to me?"

HEBREWS 13:6

———— † ————

I pray that if my pastor's heart does not condemn him, he will have confidence toward You, God.

1 JOHN 3:21

———— † ————

I pray that if my pastor will wait on You, LORD, he shall renew his strength. He shall mount up with wings like eagles. He shall run and not be weary, he shall walk and not faint.

ISAIAH 40:31

5

CONFUSED

Heavenly Father, I come now to ask You to remove
any and all confusion from my pastor. Help him to
remember at all times that Your word says You are
the author of peace and not of confusion and that
he is to lean on You and Your word and not on his
own understanding. He is one of Your chosen
servants. Be with him and give him an extra measure
of discernment and understanding and a total lack
of confusion. Thank You, in Jesus' name, for
answering these my prayers for my pastor. Amen.

God, in accordance
with Your word . . .

I pray that my pastor will trust in You, LORD,
with all his heart, and lean not on his own
understanding. I pray that in all his ways
he will acknowledge You, and You shall
direct his paths.

PROVERBS 3:5–6

I pray that You, God, will instruct my pastor and teach him in the way he should go.

PSALM 32:8

———— † ————

I pray that my pastor has great peace because he loves Your law, and nothing can cause him to stumble.

PSALM 119:165

———— † ————

I pray that my pastor will always cast his burdens on You, LORD, and You shall sustain him.

PSALM 55:22

———— † ————

I pray that when my pastor passes through the waters, You will be with him. And when he passes through the rivers, they shall not overflow him. When he walks through the fire, he shall not be burned, nor shall the flame scorch him. For You are the Lord his God.

ISAIAH 43:2–3

I pray that my pastor will be anxious for nothing, but in everything by prayer and supplication, with thanksgiving, let his requests be made known to You, God, and the peace of God, which surpasses all understanding, will guard his heart and mind through Christ Jesus.

PHILIPPIANS 4:6–7

†

I pray that my pastor will always remember that God gives power to the weak, and to those who have no might He increases strength.

ISAIAH 40:29

†

I pray that my pastor knows that where envy and self-seeking exist, confusion and every evil thing will be there. But the wisdom that is from above is first pure, then peaceable, gentle, willing to yield, full of mercy and good fruits, without partiality and without hypocrisy.

JAMES 3:16–17

I pray that You have not given my pastor a
spirit of fear, but of power and of love and
of a sound mind.

2 TIMOTHY 1:7

———— † ————

I pray that when my pastor feels confused
he will remember and understand that You,
God, are not the author of confusion but
of peace.

1 CORINTHIANS 14:33

———— † ————

I pray that my pastor will not think it strange
concerning the fiery trial which is to try him,
as though some strange thing happened to
him; but that he will rejoice to the extent
that he partakes of Christ's sufferings, that
when His glory is revealed, he may also be
glad with exceeding joy.

1 PETER 4:12–13

I pray that You, Lord God, will help my
pastor; therefore he will not be disgraced.

ISAIAH 50:7

——————— † ———————

I pray that if my pastor lacks wisdom, let
him ask of You, God, who gives to all
liberally and without reproach, and it will
be given to him.

JAMES 1:5

6
COURAGE

Jesus, grant my pastor more courage than he ever thought he would have. Help him to face trying situations with the kind of courage that comes only from You. Help him to remember that You said in Joshua that he is to be strong and of good courage. Thank You, God, in Jesus' name, for filling my pastor with courage. Amen.

God, in accordance with Your word . . .

I pray that my pastor will always fear not, for You, God, are with him. I pray that he will be not dismayed, for You are his God. I pray that You will strengthen him and help him and that You will uphold him with Your righteous right hand.

ISAIAH 41:10

I pray that my pastor will be persuaded
that neither death nor life, nor angels nor
principalities nor powers, nor things present
nor things to come, nor height nor depth,
nor any other created thing, shall be able
to separate him from the love of God which
is in Christ Jesus his Lord.

ROMANS 8:38–39

———— † ————

I pray that my pastor shall not die, but live,
and declare the works of the LORD.

PSALM 118:17

———— † ————

I pray that You, the eternal God, are my
pastor's refuge, and that You will thrust out
the enemy from before him.

DEUTERONOMY 33:27

———— † ————

I pray that my pastor can do all things
through You, Christ, who strengthen him.

PHILIPPIANS 4:13

I pray that my pastor will wait on You, LORD;
that he will be of good courage, and You
shall strengthen his heart.

PSALM 27:14

✝

I pray that my pastor does not think it
strange concerning the fiery trial which is
to try him, as though some strange thing
happened to him; but that he will rejoice
to the extent that he partakes of Christ's
sufferings, that when His glory is revealed,
he may also be glad with exceeding joy.

1 PETER 4:12–13

✝

I pray that when my pastor passes through
the waters, You will be with him; and through
the rivers, they shall not overflow him. When
he walks through the fire, he shall not be
burned, nor shall the flame scorch him.

ISAIAH 43:2

I pray that while my pastor's weeping may endure for a night, joy comes to him in the morning.

PSALM 30:5

———— † ————

I pray that my pastor will be of good courage, and that You shall strengthen his heart, for his hope is in You, LORD.

PSALM 31:24

———— † ————

I pray that my pastor will wait on You, LORD, and that he shall renew his strength. I pray that he shall mount up with wings like eagles; that he shall run and not be weary; that he shall walk and not faint.

ISAIAH 40:31

———— † ————

I pray that my pastor shall obtain joy and gladness and that sorrow and sighing shall flee away.

ISAIAH 51:11

I pray that my pastor will be anxious for nothing, but in everything by prayer and supplication, with thanksgiving, will let his requests be made known to You, God.

PHILIPPIANS 4:6

— † —

I pray that whatever things are true, whatever things are noble, whatever things are just, whatever things are pure, whatever things are lovely, whatever things are of good report, if there is any virtue and if there is anything praiseworthy—that my pastor will meditate on these things.

PHILIPPIANS 4:8

7

DELIVERANCE

Lord Jesus, I ask You to deliver my pastor from anything that might exist in his life that is unpleasing to You in any way. Set him free from all that is upon him. Thank You for the privilege of praying for my pastor and for knowing that You answer my prayers. In Your name I pray. Amen.

God, in accordance with Your word . . .

I pray that my pastor shall know the truth, and the truth shall make him free.

JOHN 8:32

---------- † ----------

I pray that if You, Jesus, make my pastor free, he shall be free indeed.

JOHN 8:36

I pray that there is therefore now no condemnation to my pastor who is in Christ Jesus, who does not walk according to the flesh, but according to the Spirit. For the law of the Spirit of life in Christ Jesus has made him free from the law of sin and death.

ROMANS 8:1–2

†

I pray that my pastor does not believe every spirit, but that he tests the spirits, whether they are of You, God; because many false prophets have gone out into the world. I pray that by this he will know the Spirit of God: that every spirit that confesses that Jesus Christ has come in the flesh is of God.

1 JOHN 4:1–2

†

I pray that He who is in my pastor is greater than he who is in the world.

1 JOHN 4:4

I pray that my pastor has overcome Satan by the blood of the Lamb and by the word of his testimony.

REVELATION 12:11

8

DEPRESSED

Heavenly Father, I ask You in Jesus' name to remove any and all depression that may at any time come upon my pastor. While I may not know if he is besieged with depression I do know that in almost every case depression is an attack from the enemy and that You have the power to remove it from him. Please honor Your word by honoring these my prayers on my pastor's behalf. Amen.

**God, in accordance
with Your word . . .**

I pray that my righteous pastor will cry out,
and You will hear and deliver him out of
all of his troubles.

PSALM 34:17

———— † ————

I pray that You are the God of my pastor's
strength.

PSALM 43:2

I pray that while my pastor's weeping may endure for a night, his joy comes in the morning.

PSALM 30:5

———— † ————

I pray that my pastor will wait on You, LORD. That he shall renew his strength. That he shall mount up with wings like eagles; that he shall run and not be weary, and that he shall walk and not faint.

ISAIAH 40:31

———— † ————

I pray that You will comfort my pastor in all his tribulation, that he may be able to comfort those who are in any trouble, with the comfort with which he himself is comforted by You.

2 CORINTHIANS 1:4

———— † ————

I pray that my pastor will not sorrow, for the joy of the LORD is his strength.

NEHEMIAH 8:10

I pray that neither death nor life, nor angels nor principalities nor powers, nor things present nor things to come, nor height nor depth, nor any other created thing, shall be able to separate my pastor from Your love, God, which is in Christ Jesus his Lord.

ROMANS 8:38–39

†

I pray that my pastor does not think it strange concerning the fiery trial which is to try him, as though some strange thing happened to him; but that he will rejoice to the extent that he partakes of Christ's suffering, so that when His glory is revealed, he may also be glad with exceeding joy.

1 PETER 4:12–13

†

I pray that my pastor will humble himself under the mighty hand of God, that You may exalt him in due time. I pray that he will cast all his cares upon You, for You care for him.

1 PETER 5:6–7

I pray that my pastor will always pray and not lose heart.

LUKE 18:1

———— † ————

I pray that whatever things are true, whatever things are noble, whatever things are just, whatever things are pure, whatever things are lovely, whatever things are of good report, if there is any virtue and if there is anything praiseworthy—that my pastor will meditate on these things.

PHILIPPIANS 4:8

———— † ————

I pray that my pastor will fear not, for You are with him. That he will be not dismayed, for You are his God. I pray that You will strengthen him; that You will help him and that You will uphold him with Your righteous right hand.

ISAIAH 41:10

I pray that You, God, will heal my pastor's broken heart and bind up his wounds.

PSALM 147:3

9

DESERTED BY LOVED ONES

Heavenly Father, if my pastor ever feels that those who love him have deserted him, help him to remember that Your word has promised that You will never leave him or forsake him, no matter what his loved ones might do. Should he ever experience those feelings I ask that You draw him close to You and remove those feelings from him. In Your Son Jesus' name I pray. Amen.

God, in accordance with Your word . . .

I pray that because You have set Your love upon my pastor, therefore You will deliver him. You will set him on high, because he has known Your name. I pray that he shall call upon You, and You will answer him. That You will be with him in trouble. That You

will deliver him and honor him. That with
long life You will satisfy him and show him
Your salvation.

PSALM 91:14–16

✝

I pray that You will not forsake my pastor
nor destroy him.

DEUTERONOMY 4:31

✝

I pray that You, God, will hear my pastor
and that You will not forsake him.

ISAIAH 41:17

✝

I pray that my pastor will cast all his cares
upon You, God, for You care for him.

1 PETER 5:7

✝

I pray that my pastor will no longer be
termed Forsaken . . . for You delight in him.

ISAIAH 62:4

I pray that while my pastor is hard pressed on every side, yet he is not crushed; he is perplexed, but not in despair; persecuted, but not forsaken; struck down, but not destroyed—always carrying about in his body the dying of the Lord Jesus, that the life of Jesus also may be manifested in his body.

2 CORINTHIANS 4:8–10

—————— † ——————

I pray that because my pastor knows Your name, God, he will put his trust in You; for You, LORD, have not forsaken those who seek You.

PSALM 9:10

—————— † ——————

I pray that my pastor will be taught to observe all things that Jesus has commanded and that he knows that You are with him always, even to the end of the age.

MATTHEW 28:20

I pray that if my pastor's father and mother forsake him that You will take care of him.

PSALM 27:10

———— † ————

I pray that my pastor's hope is in You, God, and that he shall yet praise You, the help of his countenance and his God.

PSALM 43:5

———— † ————

I pray that my pastor will be strong and of good courage. That he will not fear nor be afraid; for You, the LORD his God, are the One who goes with him. I know that You will not leave him nor forsake him.

DEUTERONOMY 31:6

———— † ————

I pray that You will not forsake my pastor, for Your great name's sake, because it has pleased You to make him one of Your people.

1 SAMUEL 12:22

10

DISCOURAGED

God, my pastor is human, and discouragement can be a factor in his life in the same way that it can be a factor in my life. Help him to overcome the inevitable setbacks that occur in all of our lives and not to become discouraged. Strengthen him and help him to remember that all things work together for good to those that love the Lord. Thank You, in Jesus' name. Amen.

God, in accordance with Your word . . .

I pray that my pastor will wait on You, LORD; that he will be of good courage and that You will strengthen his heart.

PSALM 27:14

———————— † ————————

I pray that my pastor will be of good courage, and that You, God, shall strengthen his heart.

PSALM 31:24

I pray that my pastor shall obtain joy and gladness and that sorrow and sighing shall flee away.

ISAIAH 51:11

---------- † ----------

I pray that my pastor will not cast away his confidence, which has great reward. For he has need of endurance, so that after he has done Your will, God, he may receive his promise.

HEBREWS 10:35–36

---------- † ----------

I pray that my pastor is confident of this very thing, that You, God, who have begun a good work in him will complete it until the day of Jesus Christ.

PHILIPPIANS 1:6

---------- † ----------

I pray that my pastor does not grow weary while doing good, for in due season he shall reap if he does not lose heart.

GALATIANS 6:9

I pray that my pastor will greatly rejoice,
though now for a little while, if need be, he
may be grieved by various trials. I pray that
the genuineness of his faith, being much
more precious than gold that perishes,
though it is tested by fire, may be found to
praise, honor, and glory at the revelation
of Jesus Christ, whom having not seen, he
loves. Though now he does not see Him,
yet believing, he rejoices with joy
inexpressible and full of glory, receiving the
end of his faith—the salvation of his soul.

1 PETER 1:6–9

✝

I pray that in everything my pastor will be
anxious for nothing, but in everything by
prayer and supplication, with thanksgiving,
he will let his request be made known to
You, God; and Your peace, which surpasses
all understanding, will guard his heart and
mind through Christ Jesus.

PHILIPPIANS 4:6–7

I pray, God, that though my pastor walks in the midst of trouble, You will revive him. You will stretch out Your hand against the wrath of his enemies. I pray that with Your right hand You will save him.

PSALM 138:7

———— † ————

I pray that my pastor will not let his heart be troubled. That he will believe in You, God, and also in Jesus.

JOHN 14:1

———— † ————

I pray that while my pastor is hard pressed on every side, he is not crushed; he is perplexed, but not in despair; persecuted, but not forsaken; struck down, but not destroyed—always carrying about in his body the dying of the Lord Jesus, that the life of Jesus also may be manifested in his body.

2 CORINTHIANS 4:8–10

I pray that my pastor will always understand and believe Your promise, Jesus, that Your peace You left with him and that Your peace You gave to him; and that not as the world gives did You give it to him. Let not his heart be troubled, neither let it be afraid.

JOHN 14:27

11

DISSATISFIED

Lord Jesus, please don't ever let my pastor become dissatisfied to the point that his ministry is adversely affected. Help him to remember and understand what Paul said about being content no matter what the circumstances. Help me to be a source of encouragement to him. Motivate him to be his best but not to be overly disappointed when he doesn't achieve all that he wants to. Motivate him and keep him excited about his ministry. In Your name I pray. Amen.

**God, in accordance
with Your word . . .**

I pray that You, God, who supplies seed to the sower, and bread for food, will supply and multiply the seed my pastor has sown and will increase the fruit of his righteousness.

2 CORINTHIANS 9:10

I pray that my pastor can do all things
through Christ who strengthens him.

PHILIPPIANS 4:13

---------- † ----------

I pray that my pastor's soul shall be satisfied
as with marrow and fatness, and his mouth
shall praise You with joyful lips.

PSALM 63:5

---------- † ----------

I pray that my pastor will be satisfied with
good by the fruit of his mouth.

PROVERBS 12:14

---------- † ----------

I pray that because my pastor seeks You,
Lord, he shall not lack any good thing.

PSALM 34:10

---------- † ----------

I pray that my pastor will delight himself in
You, LORD, and You shall give him the desires
of his heart.

PSALM 37:4

I pray that my pastor will bless You, Lord, with all that is within him, and that he will forget not all Your benefits. I pray that he will not forget who forgives all his iniquities and who heals all his diseases. I pray that he will not forget who redeems his life from destruction and who crowns him with lovingkindness and tender mercies, and who satisfies his mouth with good things, so that his youth is renewed like the eagle's.

PSALM 103:1–5

———— † ————

I pray that You will satisfy my pastor's longing soul and fill his hungry soul with goodness.

PSALM 107:9

———— † ————

I pray that my pastor will trust and not be afraid; for You, God, are his strength and his song.

ISAIAH 12:2

12

DISTRESS / SADNESS

Lord God in heaven, the comfort of the Holy Spirit is a promise that Jesus made to His followers. I ask You for a special comforting for my pastor during those times of distress or sadness in his life. Your word promises that even though sadness may sometimes come upon him, You will see that his joy returns in the morning. I pray that for my pastor. Thank You in advance for answering these prayers. Amen.

God, in accordance with Your word . . .

I pray that my pastor has done justice and righteousness and that You will not leave him to his oppressors.

PSALM 119:121

———————— † ————————

I pray that while my pastor may be despised, he does not forget Your precepts.

PSALM 119:141

I pray that while trouble and anguish have overtaken my pastor, Your commandments are his delights. The righteousness of Your testimonies is everlasting. I pray that You will give him understanding, and he shall live.

PSALM 119:143–144

———— † ————

I pray that in righteousness my pastor shall be established. That he shall be far from oppression, for he shall not fear; and from terror, for it shall not come near him.

ISAIAH 54:14

———— † ————

I pray that You, God, will strengthen my pastor according to Your word.

PSALM 119:28

———— † ————

I pray that it is good for my pastor that he has been afflicted, so that he may learn Your statutes.

PSALM 119:71

I pray that You, God, will consider my pastor's affliction and deliver him, for he does not forget Your law. I pray that You will plead his cause and redeem him. Revive him according to Your word.

PSALM 119:153–154

†

I pray that my pastor has great peace because he loves Your law, God, and that nothing causes him to stumble.

PSALM 119:165

†

I pray that if my pastor has gone astray like a lost sheep; that You, God, will seek him, Your servant, and not let him forget Your commandments.

PSALM 119:176

†

I pray that my pastor will always pray, "Blessed be the Lord," who daily loads him with benefits.

PSALM 68:19

I pray that You will bring my pastor up out
of a horrible pit and out of the miry clay.
Set his feet upon a rock, and establish his
steps.

PSALM 40:2

✝

I pray that You, God, are my pastor's refuge
and strength, a very present help in trouble
and that he will not fear.

PSALM 46:1–2

✝

I pray that since Your name, LORD, is a strong
tower, my righteous pastor runs to it and is
safe.

PROVERBS 18:10

✝

I pray that my pastor will let not his heart
be troubled and that he will always believe
in God and in Jesus.

JOHN 14:1

I pray that my pastor will not sorrow, for the joy of the LORD is his strength.

NEHEMIAH 8:10

———— † ————

I pray that my pastor will always live with the realization that his Lord is faithful and will establish him and guard him from the evil one.

2 THESSALONIANS 3:3

13

DON'T UNDERSTAND GOD

God, please help my pastor always to remember that Your thoughts are higher than his thoughts and that he may not always understand Your thoughts and Your ways. Remind him of Your promise that if he will call upon You, You will tell him great and unsearchable things that he does not know. I pray, on behalf of my pastor, Your word in Jesus' name. Amen.

**God, in accordance
with Your word . . .**

I pray that You, God, will help my pastor
to understand that Your thoughts are not
his thoughts, nor are his ways Your ways.
That he will understand that as the heavens
are higher than the earth, so are Your ways
higher than his ways, and Your thoughts
higher than his thoughts.

ISAIAH 55:8–9

I pray that my pastor will call to You, God, and that You will answer him and show him great and mighty things, which he does not know.

JEREMIAH 33:3

———— † ————

I pray that if You, God, are for my pastor, who can be against him?

ROMANS 8:31

———— † ————

I pray that in all things my pastor is more than a conqueror through Him who loved him.

ROMANS 8:37

———— † ————

I pray that my pastor will pursue the knowledge of the LORD.

HOSEA 6:3

I pray that as for You, God, Your way is perfect. The word of the LORD is proven; You are a shield to my pastor who trusts in You.

PSALM 18:30

---------- † ----------

I pray that You will perfect that which concerns my pastor and that Your mercy, O LORD, endures forever.

PSALM 138:8

---------- † ----------

I pray that You, God, will make an everlasting covenant with my pastor, that You will not turn away from doing him good; but that You will put Your fear in his heart so that he will not depart from You.

JEREMIAH 32:40

---------- † ----------

I pray that my pastor will hold fast the confession of his hope without wavering, for You, God, who promised are faithful.

HEBREWS 10:23

I pray that all things work together for good to my pastor who loves You, God, to him who was called according to Your purpose.

ROMANS 8:28

---

†

I pray that no temptation has overtaken my pastor except such as is common to man; but You, God, are faithful, who will not allow him to be tempted beyond what he is able, but with the temptation You will also make the way of escape, that he may be able to bear it.

1 CORINTHIANS 10:13

---

†

I pray that while many are the afflictions of my righteous pastor, You, LORD, deliver him out of them all.

PSALM 34:19

---

†

I pray that my pastor will cast his burden on You, LORD, and You shall sustain him.

PSALM 55:22

I pray that my pastor will fear not, for You, God, are with him. That he will be not dismayed, for You are his God. That You will strengthen him and help him. That You will uphold him with Your righteous right hand.

ISAIAH 41:10

———————— † ————————

I pray that my pastor does not think it strange concerning the fiery trial which is to try him, as though some strange thing happened to him. But that he will rejoice to the extent that he partakes of Christ's sufferings, that when His glory is revealed, he may also be glad with exceeding joy.

1 PETER 4:12–13

14

DOUBTING GOD

Heavenly Father, I cannot imagine that my pastor
would ever doubt anything about You or anything
You told him to do. But out of love for him and his
obedience to you I ask You now to remove from
him any doubts that he might ever have about You
or Your word or Your calling of him to be a pastor
and a minister of Your word. Keep the enemy away
from him and prevent him from planting seeds of
doubt in my pastor's mind. Honor the prayers that
come directly from Your word so that he may be
full of confidence and free from doubt. In Jesus'
name I pray. Amen.

**God, in accordance
with Your word . . .**

I pray that because Your way is perfect and
Your word is proven; that You, God, are a
shield to my pastor who trusts in You.

PSALM 18:30

I pray that my pastor will always remember
that Your hand is not shortened so that it
cannot save; nor Your ear heavy, that it
cannot hear.

ISAIAH 59:1

---------- † ----------

I pray that You, Lord, are not slack
concerning Your promise, as some count
slackness, but are longsuffering toward my
pastor, not willing that he should perish but
that he should come to repentance.

2 PETER 3:9

---------- † ----------

I pray that my pastor does not seek what
he should eat or what he should drink, nor
have an anxious mind. For all these things
the nations of the world seek after, and You,
his Father, know that he needs these things.
I pray that he will seek the kingdom of God,
and all these things shall be added to him.

LUKE 12:29–31

I pray that my pastor is aware that You have said Your counsel shall stand, and You will do all Your pleasure. Indeed, You have spoken it and You will also bring it to pass. You have purposed it and You will also do it.

ISAIAH 46:10–11

———— † ————

I pray that my pastor knows that He who calls him is faithful, who also will do it.

1 THESSALONIANS 5:24

———— † ————

I pray that my pastor will always remember that You, God, have declared that, "So shall My word be that goes forth from My mouth; it shall not return to Me void, but it shall accomplish what I please, and it shall prosper in the thing for which I sent it."

ISAIAH 55:11

———— † ————

I pray that my pastor knows that faith comes by hearing, and hearing by the word of God.

ROMANS 10:17

I pray that whatever things my pastor asks for when he prays, that he will believe that he will receive them, and he will have them.

MARK 11:24

———— † ————

I pray that my pastor does not think it strange concerning the fiery trial which is to try him, as though some strange thing happened to him. But that he rejoices to the extent that he partakes of Christ's sufferings, that when His glory is revealed, he may also be glad with exceeding joy.

1 PETER 4:12–13

15

EMOTIONALLY UPSET

Jesus, my pastor has so many difficult situations that he must deal with in our church family. I know that many of these situations must be emotionally upsetting to him. Today I want to pray Your perfect will for him in this area. Thank You in advance for answering these my prayers. Amen.

**God, in accordance
with Your word . . .**

I pray that my pastor will have great peace because he loves Your law, and nothing causes him to stumble.

PSALM 119:165

————— † —————

I pray that because my pastor believes in You, God, he will by no means be put to shame.

1 PETER 2:6

I pray that You, God, will help my pastor; therefore he will not be disgraced. He can set his face like a flint, and know that he will not be ashamed.

ISAIAH 50:7

---------- † ----------

I pray that my pastor will cast his burden on You, LORD, and that You will sustain him.

PSALM 55:22

---------- † ----------

I pray that You, God, have not given my pastor a spirit of fear, but of power and of love and of a sound mind.

2 TIMOTHY 1:7

---------- † ----------

I pray that my pastor will fear not, for You, God, are with him. That he be not dismayed, for You are his God. I pray that You will strengthen him and help him and that You will uphold him with Your righteous right hand.

ISAIAH 41:10

I pray that my pastor will be anxious for nothing, but in everything by prayer and supplication, with thanksgiving, let his requests be made known to You, God, and Your peace, God, which surpasses all understanding, will guard his heart and mind through Christ Jesus.

PHILIPPIANS 4:6–7

―――― † ――――

I pray that my pastor will realize that You, God, are not the author of confusion but of peace.

1 CORINTHIANS 14:33

―――― † ――――

I pray that my pastor knows that where envy and self-seeking exist, confusion and every evil thing are there. I pray that he will also know that the wisdom that is from above is first pure, then peaceable, gentle, willing to yield, full of mercy and good fruits, without partiality and without hypocrisy and that the fruit of righteousness is sown in peace by those who make peace.

JAMES 3:16–18

I pray that while my pastor's weeping may endure for a night, his joy comes in the morning.

PSALM 30:5

———— † ————

I pray that when my pastor passes through the waters, You, God, will be with him. And when he passes through the rivers, they shall not overflow him. I pray that when he walks through the fire, he shall not be burned, nor shall the flame scorch him. You are the Lord his God.

ISAIAH 43:2–3

———— † ————

I pray that You, God, will comfort my pastor in all his tribulation, that he may be able to comfort those who are in any trouble, with the comfort with which he himself is comforted by You.

2 CORINTHIANS 1:4

I pray that You, God, will heal my pastor's
broken heart and bind up his wounds.

PSALM 147:3

———————— † ————————

I pray that whatever things are true,
whatever things are noble, whatever things
are just, whatever things are pure, whatever
things are lovely, whatever things are of good
report, if there is any virtue and if there is
anything praiseworthy—that my pastor will
meditate on these things.

PHILIPPIANS 4:8

———————— † ————————

I pray that neither death nor life, nor angels
nor principalities nor powers, nor things
present nor things to come, nor height nor
depth, nor any other created thing, shall be
able to separate my pastor from the love
of God which is in Christ Jesus his Lord.

ROMANS 8:38–39

16

FAITH

Heavenly Father, my pastor is a man of faith. And I thank You for sending him to us. Please give him more faith than ever before. Reveal yourself to him in such a way that his faith is strengthened. I ask this and I thank You for it in Jesus' name. Amen.

God, in accordance with Your word . . .

I pray that You, Lord, will increase my pastor's faith.

LUKE 17:5

———— † ————

I pray that my pastor's faith comes by hearing, and hearing by the word of God.

ROMANS 10:17

I pray that my pastor will walk by faith and not by sight.

2 CORINTHIANS 5:7

---- † ----

I pray that my pastor will have love from a pure heart, from a good conscience, and from sincere faith.

1 TIMOTHY 1:5

---- † ----

I pray that my pastor will always remember that faith is the substance of things hoped for, and the evidence of things not seen.

HEBREWS 11:1

---- † ----

I pray that my pastor will constantly take the shield of faith with which he will be able to quench all the fiery darts of the wicked one.

EPHESIANS 6:16

I pray that my pastor remembers that faith by itself, if it does not have works, is dead.

JAMES 2:17

———— † ————

I pray that my pastor will put on the breastplate of faith and love, and as his helmet the hope of salvation.

1 THESSALONIANS 5:8

———— † ————

I pray that my pastor will always have faith and a good conscience.

1 TIMOTHY 1:19

———— † ————

I pray that my pastor will draw near with a true heart in full assurance of his faith and that he will have his heart sprinkled from an evil conscience and his body washed with pure water.

HEBREWS 10:22

I pray that my pastor will fight the good fight
of faith, that he will lay hold on eternal life,
to which he was also called.

1 TIMOTHY 6:12

—————— ✝ ——————

I pray that my pastor understands that
without faith it is impossible to please You,
God, and that for him to come to You he
must believe that You are, and that You are
a rewarder of those who diligently seek You.

HEBREWS 11:6

—————— ✝ ——————

I pray that my pastor will be just and will
live by faith.

HABAKKUK 2:4

—————— ✝ ——————

I pray that my pastor will remember that
Abraham believed God, and it was
accounted to him for righteousness.

ROMANS 4:3

I pray that my pastor, having been justified
by faith, will have peace with You, God,
through his Lord Jesus Christ.

ROMANS 5:1

---------- † ----------

I pray that my pastor will count all things
as a loss for the excellence of the knowledge
of Christ Jesus his Lord, for whom he has
suffered the loss of all things, and count
them as rubbish, that he may gain Christ
and be found in Him, not having his own
righteousness, which is from the law, but
that which is through faith in Christ, the
righteousness which is from God by faith;
that he may know Him and the power of
His resurrection, and the fellowship of His
sufferings, being conformed to His death.

PHILIPPIANS 3:8–10

---------- † ----------

I pray that my pastor will be just and will
live by faith.

HEBREWS 10:38

I pray that my pastor shall believe in You, the LORD his God, and that he shall be established. I pray also that he will believe Your prophets, and he shall prosper.

2 CHRONICLES 20:20

———— † ————

I pray that according to my pastor's faith, it will be to him.

MATTHEW 9:29

———— † ————

I pray that my pastor will have faith as a mustard seed, and he will say to his mountain, "Move from here to there," and it will move; and nothing will be impossible for him.

MATTHEW 17:20

———— † ————

I pray that my pastor will have faith in You, God.

MARK 11:22

I pray for my pastor the righteousness of You, God, which is through faith in Jesus Christ, on him who believes.

ROMANS 3:22

— ✝ —

I pray that in Your forbearance, God, You have passed over my pastor's sins that were previously committed.

ROMANS 3:25

— ✝ —

I pray that my pastor will remember that if he has the gift of prophecy, and understands all mysteries and all knowledge, and though he has all faith, so that he can remove mountains, but has not love, he is nothing.

1 CORINTHIANS 13:2

— ✝ —

I pray that my pastor will watch and that he will stand fast in the faith and that he will be brave and strong.

1 CORINTHIANS 16:13

I pray that my pastor will examine himself
as to whether he is in the faith and that he
will prove himself.

2 CORINTHIANS 13:5

✝

I pray that my pastor knows that he is not
justified by the works of the law but by faith
in Jesus Christ.

GALATIANS 2:16

✝

I pray that my pastor has been crucified with
Christ. That it is no longer he who lives, but
Christ who lives in him. And that the life
which he now lives in the flesh he lives by
faith in the Son of God, who loves him and
gave Himself for him.

GALATIANS 2:20

✝

I pray that my pastor will fight the good fight;
that he will finish the race; and that he will
keep the faith.

2 TIMOTHY 4:7

I pray that my pastor knows the Holy Scriptures, which are able to make him wise for salvation through his faith which is in Christ Jesus.

2 TIMOTHY 3:15

— † —

I pray that the sharing of my pastor's faith may become effective by the acknowledgment of every good thing which is in him in Christ Jesus.

PHILEMON 1:6

— † —

I pray that it is by faith that my pastor understands that the worlds were framed by the word of God, so that the things which are seen were not made of things which are visible.

HEBREWS 11:3

— † —

I pray that my pastor will realize that if he does not believe he shall not be established.

ISAIAH 7:9

I pray that my pastor will always look unto Jesus, the author and finisher of his faith, who for the joy that was set before Him endured the cross, despising the shame, and sat down at the right hand of the throne of God.

HEBREWS 12:2

———— † ————

I pray that my pastor understands that as the body without the spirit is dead, so faith without works is dead also.

JAMES 2:26

17

FEAR

God, at one time or another all of us experience some measure of fear. But You told us in Joshua to "fear not" and that You would never leave us or forsake us. Help my pastor to remember that whenever he experiences fear in any way. Give him courage to overcome his fear. In Jesus' name I pray. Amen.

God, in accordance with Your word . . .

I pray that Your truth, God, shall be my pastor's shield and buckler and that he shall not be afraid.

PSALM 91:4–5

✝

I pray that no evil shall befall my pastor.

PSALM 91:10

I pray that my pastor will not be afraid of sudden terror, nor of trouble from the wicked when it comes. I pray that You, LORD, will be his confidence and will keep his foot from being caught.

PROVERBS 3:25–26

I pray that in righteousness my pastor shall be established. He shall be far from oppression, for he shall not fear. And from terror, for it shall not come near him.

ISAIAH 54:14

I pray that in You, God, my pastor has put his trust and that he will not be afraid.

PSALM 56:11

I pray that my pastor knows that You, God, have not given him a spirit of fear, but of power and of love and of a sound mind.

2 TIMOTHY 1:7

I pray that my pastor did not receive the spirit of bondage again to fear, but that he received the Spirit of adoption by whom he cries out, "Abba, Father."

ROMANS 8:15

———— † ————

I pray that in my pastor there is no fear in love; because perfect love casts out fear.

1 JOHN 4:18

———— † ————

I pray that You, God, will give Your angels charge over my pastor, to keep him in all his ways.

PSALM 91:11

———— † ————

I pray that though my pastor walks through the valley of the shadow of death, he will fear no evil; for You, God, are with him. Your rod and Your staff, they comfort him.

PSALM 23:4

I pray that if You, God, are for my pastor, who can be against him? Who shall separate him from the love of Christ? Shall tribulation, or distress, or persecution, or famine, or nakedness, or peril, or sword? I pray that in all these things he is more than a conqueror through Him who loved him. For I am persuaded that neither death nor life, nor angels nor principalities nor powers, nor things present nor things to come, nor height nor depth, nor any other created thing, shall be able to separate my pastor from Your love, God, which is in Christ Jesus his Lord.

ROMANS 8:31, 35, 37–39

——— † ———

I pray that my pastor will be of good courage and that You, God, shall strengthen his heart for his hope is in the LORD.

PSALM 31:24

——— † ———

I pray that You, Lord, are my pastor's helper and that he will not fear.

HEBREWS 13:6

I pray that my pastor receives the peace that
You, Jesus, have left with him, the peace You
gave to him. Let not his heart be troubled,
neither let it be afraid.

JOHN 14:27

———— † ————

I pray that You, LORD, are my pastor's light
and his salvation. Whom shall he fear?
Though an army may encamp against him,
his heart shall not fear. In this he will be
confident.

PSALM 27:1, 3

18

FINANCIAL PROBLEMS

Heavenly Father, all of us, pastors included, have to deal with financial problems on a regular basis. At times they can be time consuming and mentally draining. My prayers to You now are that You will keep my pastor and my church from financial problems. Shield them from those problems so that they can be about the work that You have for them to do. Thank You, Father, in Jesus' name. Amen.

God, in accordance
with Your word . . .

I pray that my pastor may prosper in all things and be in health, just as his soul prospers.

3 JOHN 1:2

———— † ————

I pray that You, LORD, are my pastor's shepherd and that he shall not want.

PSALM 23:1

I pray that my pastor will seek You, LORD, and not lack any good thing.

PSALM 34:10

---------- † ----------

I pray that all these blessings shall come upon my pastor and overtake him, because he obeys the voice of the LORD his God. He shall be blessed in the city and he shall be blessed in the country. He shall be blessed when he comes in and he shall be blessed when he goes out. I pray that You, LORD, will command Your blessing on him in his storehouses and in all to which he sets his hand.

DEUTERONOMY 28:2–3, 6, 8

---------- † ----------

I pray that my pastor will give, and it will be given to him: good measure, pressed down, shaken together, and running over will be put into his bosom. For with the same measure that he uses, it will be measured back to him.

LUKE 6:38

I pray that freely my pastor has received,
freely he will give.

MATTHEW 10:8

———— † ————

I pray that on the first day of the week my
pastor will lay something aside, storing up
as he may prosper, so that there be no
collections when it is time to give.

1 CORINTHIANS 16:2

———— † ————

I pray that my pastor realizes that if he
sows sparingly he will also reap sparingly
and if he sows bountifully he will also reap
bountifully. I pray that he will give as he
purposes in his heart, not grudgingly or of
necessity; for You, God, love a cheerful giver.
And You are able to make all grace abound
toward him, that my pastor, always having
all sufficiency in all things, may have an
abundance for every good work.

2 CORINTHIANS 9:6–8

I pray that my pastor will bring all his tithes into the storehouse, that there may be food in God's house. And that he will try You, God, in this and see if You will not open for him the windows of heaven and pour out for him such blessing that there will not be room enough to receive it.

MALACHI 3:10

———— † ————

I pray that this Book of the Law shall not depart from my pastor's mouth, but he shall meditate in it day and night, that he may observe to do according to all that is written in it. For then he will make his way prosperous, and then he will have good success.

JOSHUA 1:8

———— † ————

I pray that You, God, shall supply all my pastor's needs according to Your riches in glory by Christ Jesus.

PHILIPPIANS 4:19

I pray that You will give wisdom and knowledge and joy to my pastor who is good in Your sight. But to the sinner You will give the work of gathering and collecting, that he may give to my pastor who is good before You.

ECCLESIASTES 2:26

———— † ————

I pray that my pastor leaves an inheritance to his children's children.

PROVERBS 13:22

———— † ————

I pray that my pastor does not worry, saying, "What shall I eat?" or "What shall I drink?" or "What shall I wear?" For You, his Heavenly Father, know that he needs all these things. But I pray that he will seek first Your kingdom, God, and Your righteousness, and all these things shall be added to him. I also pray that he does not worry about tomorrow, for tomorrow will worry about its own things.

MATTHEW 6:31-34

I pray that my pastor will remember that everyone who has left houses or brothers or sisters or father or mother or wife or children or lands for Your name's sake, Lord, shall receive a hundredfold, and inherit eternal life. I pray also that my pastor will remember that many who are first will be last, and the last first.

MATTHEW 19:29–30

19

FORGIVENESS

Lord God, all of us make mistakes for which we need forgiveness. Because my pastor is human he, too, makes mistakes and needs forgiveness. I ask You now to forgive him when forgiveness is in order and to help him to be aware of his need for and his receipt of forgiveness. In Jesus' name I make this request. Amen.

**God, in accordance
with Your word . . .**

I pray that as far as the east is from the west, so far have You, God, removed my pastor's transgressions from him.

PSALM 103:12

— ✝ —

I pray that You blot out my pastor's transgressions for Your own sake and that You will not remember his sins.

ISAIAH 43:25

I pray that my pastor will return to You, LORD, and that You will have mercy on him; and to his God, for You will abundantly pardon.

ISAIAH 55:7

---------- † ----------

I pray that You, God, will cleanse my pastor from all his iniquity by which he has sinned against You, and that You will pardon all his iniquities by which he has sinned and by which he has transgressed against You.

JEREMIAH 33:8

---------- † ----------

I pray that my pastor's transgressions are forgiven and his sin is covered.

PSALM 32:1

---------- † ----------

I pray that whenever my pastor stands praying, if he has anything against anyone that he will forgive him, so that you, his Father in heaven, may also forgive my pastor of his trespasses.

MARK 11:25

I pray that in You, Jesus, my pastor has redemption through Your blood, the forgiveness of his sins, according to the riches of God's grace which He made to abound toward him in all wisdom and prudence, having made known to him the mystery of His will, according to His good pleasure which He purposed in Himself.

EPHESIANS 1:7–9

✝

I pray that my pastor will bear with others, and forgive others, if he has a complaint against another; even as Christ forgave him, so he also must do.

COLOSSIANS 3:13

✝

I pray that if my pastor confesses his sins, that You, God, are faithful and just to forgive his sins and to cleanse him from all unrighteousness.

1 JOHN 1:9

I pray that my pastor will walk by faith and not by sight.

2 CORINTHIANS 5:7

---------- † ----------

I pray that if my pastor sins, he has an Advocate with You, the Father, Jesus Christ the righteous.

1 JOHN 2:1

20

GODLY LIFE

Lord Jesus, my pastor is a man that You have chosen to lead us and to lead our church. He is Your man for this time in our life. I ask You, God, to motivate him and encourage him to live the most godly life possible. Help him always to remember that we look to him for leadership and as an example of how You want us to live. Help him to never be less than what You desire him to be. In Your name. Amen.

God, in accordance
with Your word . . .

I pray that my pastor does not present his members as instruments of unrighteousness to sin, but presents himself to You, God, as being alive from the dead, and his members as instruments of righteousness to You. For sin shall not have dominion over him, for he is not under law but under grace.

ROMANS 6:13–14

I pray that if my pastor lives, he lives to You, Lord; and if he dies, he dies to You, Lord. Therefore, whether he lives or dies, he is Yours, Lord.

ROMANS 14:8

————— † —————

I pray that if my pastor believes on You, Jesus, who justify the ungodly, his faith is accounted for righteousness.

ROMANS 4:5

————— † —————

I pray that what the law could not do in my pastor in that it was weak through the flesh, You, God, did by sending Your own Son in the likeness of sinful flesh, on account of sin: You condemned sin in my pastor, that the righteous requirement of the law might be fulfilled in him who does not walk according to the flesh but according to the Spirit.

ROMANS 8:3–4

I pray that my pastor will present his body as a living sacrifice, holy, and acceptable to You, God.

ROMANS 12:1

---
†

I pray that my pastor will not be conformed to this world, but that he will be transformed by the renewing of his mind, that he may prove what is that good and acceptable and perfect will of God.

ROMANS 12:2

---
†

I pray that my pastor will not think of himself more highly than he ought to think, but to think soberly, as You, God, have dealt to him a measure of faith.

ROMANS 12:3

---
†

I pray that because You, Christ, are in my pastor, his body is dead because of sin, but the Spirit is life because of righteousness.

ROMANS 8:10

I pray that my pastor whom You, God, predestined, You also called; whom You called, You also justified; and whom You justified, You also glorified.

ROMANS 8:30

—————— † ——————

I pray that because my pastor is in You, Christ, he is a new creation; old things have passed away; behold, all things have become new.

2 CORINTHIANS 5:17

—————— † ——————

I pray that my pastor will remain in the same calling in which he was called.

1 CORINTHIANS 7:20

—————— † ——————

I pray that You, God, are able to make all grace abound toward my pastor, that he, always having all sufficiency in all things, may have an abundance for every good work.

2 CORINTHIANS 9:8

I pray that You, God, made Jesus who knew
no sin to be sin for my pastor, that he might
become the righteousness of You in Him.

2 CORINTHIANS 5:21

----- † -----

I pray that if my pastor glories, he will glory
in You, Lord.

1 CORINTHIANS 1:31

----- † -----

I pray that my pastor will not let sin reign
in his mortal body, that he should obey it
in its lusts.

ROMANS 6:12

----- † -----

I pray that my pastor will be renewed in the
spirit of his mind and that he will put on
his new self which was created according
to You, God, in true righteousness and
holiness.

EPHESIANS 4:23–24

I pray that my pastor has been set free from
sin and has become a slave of God.

ROMANS 6:22

---

†

I pray that it is good for my pastor to draw
near to You, God; to put his trust in the Lord
GOD, that he may declare all Your works.

PSALM 73:28

---

†

I pray that my pastor will delight himself in
You, LORD, and that You shall give him the
desires of his heart.

PSALM 37:4

---

†

I pray that You, God, will satisfy my pastor's
mouth with good things so that his youth
is renewed like the eagle's.

PSALM 103:5

I pray that You, God, are a companion to my pastor who fears You and who keeps Your precepts.

PSALM 119:63

———— † ————

I pray that my pastor, who walks in the law of the LORD, will be blessed.

PSALM 119:1

———— † ————

I pray that my pastor's ways are directed to keep Your statutes, God.

PSALM 119:5

———— † ————

I pray that with my pastor's whole heart he has sought You, God. Let him not wander from Your commandments!

PSALM 119:10

———— † ————

I pray that my pastor will cleanse his way by taking heed according to Your word, God.

PSALM 119:9

I pray that my pastor has hidden Your word
in his heart, God, that he might not sin
against You.

PSALM 119:11

---------- † ----------

I pray that my pastor will delight himself in
Your statutes, God; and that he will not forget
Your word.

PSALM 119:16

---------- † ----------

I pray that You, God, will open my pastor's
eyes, that he may see wondrous things from
Your law.

PSALM 119:18

---------- † ----------

I pray that my pastor has declared his ways
and that You, God, have answered him and
that You will teach him Your statutes.

PSALM 119:26

I pray that Your testimonies also are my
pastor's delight and his counselors.

PSALM 119:24

———— † ————

I pray that You, God, will make my pastor
understand the way of Your precepts; so shall
he meditate on Your wondrous works.

PSALM 119:27

———— † ————

I pray that my pastor has chosen the way
of truth and that Your judgments he has laid
before him. I pray that he will cling to Your
testimonies, God, and that he will not be
put to shame!

PSALM 119:30–31

———— † ————

I pray that You will make my pastor walk
in the path of Your commandments and that
he will delight in it.

PSALM 119:35

I pray that my pastor will incline his heart
to Your testimonies, God, and not to
covetousness. I pray that he will turn away
his eyes from looking at worthless things
and that You will revive him in Your way.

PSALM 119:36–37

✝

I pray that You, God, will remember the
word to my pastor, Your servant, upon which
You have caused him to hope.

PSALM 119:49

✝

I pray that You, God, will be merciful to my
pastor according to Your word.

PSALM 119:58

✝

I pray, O God, that my pastor has thought
about his ways, and has turned his feet to
Your testimonies. I pray that he has made
haste, and did not delay to keep Your
commandments.

PSALM 119:59–60

I pray that You, God, will teach my pastor
good judgment and knowledge, for he
believes Your commandments.

PSALM 119:66

———— † ————

I pray that Your hands have made my pastor
and fashioned him. Give him understanding,
that he may learn Your commandments.

PSALM 119:73

———— † ————

I pray that You will let Your merciful kindness
be for my pastor's comfort.

PSALM 119:76

———— † ————

I pray that You will let my pastor's heart be
blameless regarding Your statutes, that he
may not be ashamed.

PSALM 119:80

I pray that my pastor will never forget Your precepts, for by them You have given him life.

PSALM 119:93

———— † ————

I pray that Your word, O God, is a lamp to my pastor's feet and a light to his path.

PSALM 119:105

———— † ————

I pray that You, God, are my pastor's hiding place and his shield, and that his hope is in Your word.

PSALM 119:114

———— † ————

I pray that You, God, will give my pastor understanding that he may know Your testimonies.

PSALM 119:125

I pray that my pastor's steps are directed by Your word, God, and that You let no iniquity have dominion over him.

PSALM 119:133

———— † ————

I pray that my pastor shall love You, the Lord his God, with all his heart, with all his soul, with all his mind, and with all his strength and that he shall love his neighbor as himself.

MARK 12:30–31

———— † ————

I pray that You, Jesus, are always at my pastor's right hand, that he may not be shaken.

ACTS 2:25

———— † ————

I pray that my pastor may gain You, Christ, and be found in You, not having his own righteousness, which is from the law, but that which is through faith in You, the righteousness which is from God by faith; that he may know You and the power of Your resurrection, and the fellowship of Your sufferings, being conformed to Your death.

PHILIPPIANS 3:8–10

———— † ————

I pray that if my pastor confesses his sins, that You, God, are faithful and just to forgive his sins and to cleanse him from all unrighteousness.

1 JOHN 1:9

———— † ————

I pray that blessed is my pastor who walks not in the counsel of the ungodly, nor stands in the path of sinners, nor sits in the seat of the scornful. But his delight is in the law of the LORD, and in Your law he meditates day and night. I pray that he shall be like a tree planted by the rivers of water, that brings forth its fruit in its season, whose leaf also shall not wither; and whatever he does shall prosper.

PSALM 1:1–3

I pray that the work of my pastor's righteousness will be peace, and the effect of his righteousness, quietness and assurance forever.

ISAIAH 32:17

✝

I pray that my pastor shall know the truth and the truth shall make him free.

JOHN 8:32

✝

I pray that my pastor takes up Your whole armor, God, that he may be able to withstand in the evil day, and having done all, to stand. I pray that he will gird his waist with truth, that he will put on the breastplate of righteousness and will shoe his feet with the preparation of the gospel of peace; and above all, take the shield of faith with which he will be able to quench all the fiery darts of the wicked one. I pray that he will take the helmet of salvation, and the sword of the Spirit, which is the word of God; praying always with all prayer and supplication in the Spirit, being watchful to this end with all perseverance and supplication for all the saints.

EPHESIANS 6:13–18

———— † ————

I pray that my pastor will be diligent to present himself approved to You, God, a worker who does not need to be ashamed, rightly dividing the word of truth.

2 TIMOTHY 2:15

———— † ————

I pray that no one deceives my pastor with empty words.

EPHESIANS 5:6

———— † ————

I pray that my pastor will be a doer of the word, and not a hearer only.

JAMES 1:22

I pray that my pastor will not be deceived, for You, God, are not mocked; for whatever he sows, that he will also reap.

GALATIANS 6:7

———— † ————

I pray that my pastor always remembers that all Scripture is given by inspiration of You, God, and is profitable for doctrine, for reproof, for correction, for instruction in righteousness, that the man of God may be complete, thoroughly equipped for every good work.

2 TIMOTHY 3:16–17

21

GOD'S LOVE

Lord God, I ask You today to love my pastor in a very special way. Help him to experience Your love today and every day. Help him to sense Your love and Your closeness to him and his family. Please hear and honor Your very words that I am going to pray for my pastor. In Jesus' name I pray. Amen.

God, in accordance with Your word . . .

I pray that my pastor knows that love is not
that he loved You, God, but that You
loved him and sent Your Son to be the
propitiation for his sins.

1 JOHN 4:10

---------- † ----------

I pray that my pastor loves You, God,
because You first loved him.

1 JOHN 4:19

I pray that You, Christ, may dwell in my pastor's heart through faith and that he, being rooted and grounded in love, may be able to comprehend with all the saints what is the width and length and depth and height—to know Your love which passes knowledge; that he may be filled with all the fullness of God.

EPHESIANS 3:17–19

———— † ————

I pray that my pastor never forgets that You, God, demonstrated Your own love toward him, in that while he was still a sinner, Christ died for him.

ROMANS 5:8

———— † ————

I pray that You, God, so loved my pastor that You gave Your only begotten Son, that my pastor who believes in Him should not perish but have everlasting life.

JOHN 3:16

I pray that neither death nor life, nor angels nor principalities nor powers, nor things present nor things to come, nor height nor depth, nor any other created thing, shall be able to separate my pastor from the love of You, God, which is in Christ Jesus his Lord.

ROMANS 8:38–39

✝

I pray that my pastor has Your commandments and keeps them and loves You. And because he loves You he will be loved by You, and You will love him and manifest Yourself to him.

JOHN 14:21

✝

I pray that my pastor knows that You, God, have loved him with an everlasting love and with lovingkindness You have drawn him.

JEREMIAH 31:3

I pray that my pastor realizes that You, God,
will rejoice over him with gladness. That
You will quiet him with Your love and
that You will rejoice over him with singing.

ZEPHANIAH 3:17

22
GOD'S WORD

Heavenly Father, Your word is our way of knowing You. This very day I want to pray Your actual words to You and in so doing pray that more than ever before Your word will live within my pastor's heart. Please instill Your word in him in a powerful way. Thank You, in Jesus' name. Amen.

God, in accordance with Your word . . .

I pray that in my pastor's life Your word is living and powerful, and sharper than any two-edged sword, piercing even to the division of his soul and spirit, and of his joints and marrow, and that it is a discerner of the thoughts and intents of his heart.

HEBREWS 4:12

———— † ————

I pray that my pastor never forgets that the word of the Lord endures forever.

1 PETER 1:25

I pray that my pastor has been born again,
not of corruptible seed but incorruptible,
through Your word, God, which lives and
abides forever.

1 PETER 1:23

———— † ————

I pray that my pastor puts into practice the
fact that he shall not live by bread alone,
but by every word that proceeds from the
mouth of God.

MATTHEW 4:4

———— † ————

I pray that my pastor will always understand
and apply the fact that all Scripture is given
by Your inspiration, God, and is profitable
for doctrine, for reproof, for correction, for
instruction in righteousness, that he may be
complete, thoroughly equipped for every
good work.

2 TIMOTHY 3:16–17

I pray that my pastor knows that he has been given exceedingly great and precious promises, that through these he may be a partaker of the divine nature, having escaped the corruption that is in the world through lust.

2 PETER 1:4

———— † ————

I pray that my pastor always remembers that heaven and earth will pass away, but Jesus' words will by no means pass away.

MATTHEW 24:35

———— † ————

I pray that my pastor understands the significance of the fact that until heaven and earth pass away, one jot or one tittle will by no means pass from the law till all is fulfilled.

MATTHEW 5:18

I pray that my pastor takes to heart the fact that heaven and earth will pass away, but Your words, Jesus, will by no means pass away.

MARK 13:31

✝

I pray that if my pastor will abide in Your words, Jesus, he is indeed Your disciple. And if he does that he shall know the truth and the truth shall make him free.

JOHN 8:31–32

✝

I pray that my pastor's walk with You, Lord, will be so close that his ears shall hear a word behind him, saying, "This is the way, walk in it."

ISAIAH 30:21

✝

I pray that my pastor realizes the significance of the fact that You, God, said, "So shall My word be that goes forth from My mouth; it shall not return to Me void."

ISAIAH 55:11

I pray that You, O God, will instruct my pastor and teach him in the way he should go and that You will guide him with Your eye.

PSALM 32:8

———— † ————

I pray that my pastor will not be like the horse or the mule, which have no understanding but must be controlled by bit and bridle or they will not come to You.

PSALM 32:9

———— † ————

I pray that my pastor will take Your testimonies as a heritage forever, for they are the rejoicing of his heart.

PSALM 119:111

———— † ————

I pray that my pastor is Your servant, O God, and that You will give him understanding, that he may know Your testimonies.

PSALM 119:125

I pray that my pastor will give attention to Your words, O God, that he will incline his ear to Your sayings. Do not let them depart from his eyes and keep them in the midst of his heart, for they are life to him when he finds them, and health to all his flesh.

PROVERBS 4:20–22

————— † —————

I pray that my pastor will know that every word of God is pure and that You are a shield to those who put their trust in You. I pray that he will not add to Your words, lest You reprove him, and he be found a liar.

PROVERBS 30:5–6

————— † —————

I pray that my pastor will not let Your Book of the Law depart from his mouth, but he shall meditate in it day and night, that he may observe to do according to all that is written in it. For then he will make his way prosperous, and then he will have good success.

JOSHUA 1:8

23
GRIEF / HURTING

God, more than most of us, my pastor understands the meaning of grief and the pain of hurting. As I pray Your words for him, please anoint him with a special understanding of how these prayers also can minister to others during their times of pain and grief. Thank You, in Jesus' name, for using Your words to comfort others. Amen.

God, in accordance
with Your word . . .

I pray that my pastor is blessed when he mourns for he shall be comforted.

MATTHEW 5:4

———— † ————

I pray that my pastor will not be ignorant concerning those who have fallen asleep, lest he sorrow as others who have no hope.

1 THESSALONIANS 4:13

I pray that You, God, will console my pastor who mourns and give him beauty for ashes, the oil of joy for mourning, the garment of praise for the spirit of heaviness so that he may be called a tree of righteousness.

ISAIAH 61:3

--- † ---

I pray, O God, that You will comfort my pastor in all his tribulations, that he may be able to comfort those who are in any trouble, with the comfort with which he himself is comforted by You.

2 CORINTHIANS 1:4

--- † ---

I pray that when my pastor passes through the waters, You, God, will be with him, and when he passes through the rivers, they shall not overflow him. When he walks through the fire, he shall not be burned, nor shall the flame scorch him.

ISAIAH 43:2

I pray, O God, that You have comforted my pastor and will have mercy on his affliction.

ISAIAH 49:13

———— † ————

I pray that the Lord Jesus Christ Himself and You, God, who have loved my pastor and given him everlasting consolation and good hope by grace, will comfort his heart and establish him in every good word and work.

2 THESSALONIANS 2:16–17

———— † ————

I pray that my pastor always remembers that in You, Jesus, he does not have a High Priest who cannot sympathize with his weaknesses, but was in all points tempted as he is, yet without sin. Let him therefore come boldly to the throne of grace, that he may obtain mercy and find grace to help in time of need.

HEBREWS 4:15–16

I pray that though my pastor may walk through the valley of the shadow of death, he will fear no evil; for You, God, are with him and Your rod and Your staff, they comfort him.

PSALM 23:4

✝

I pray that in this crucial time in my pastor's life he can say, "O Death, where is your sting? O Hades, where is your victory?"

1 CORINTHIANS 15:55

✝

I pray that this is my pastor's comfort in his affliction, that Your word, God, has given him life.

PSALM 119:50

✝

I pray that my pastor will cast all his cares upon You, O God, for You care for him.

1 PETER 5:7

I pray that You, God, will wipe away every tear from my pastor's eyes and that there shall be no more death, nor sorrow, nor crying. I pray that there shall be no more pain, for the former things have passed away.

REVELATION 21:4

---------- † ----------

I pray that my pastor will fear not, for You, God, are with him. I pray that he will not be dismayed, for You are his God. I pray that You will strengthen him and help him and that You will uphold him with Your righteous right hand.

ISAIAH 41:10

---------- † ----------

I pray that my pastor shall obtain joy and gladness and that sorrow and sighing shall flee away.

ISAIAH 51:11

I pray that my pastor will walk by faith and not by sight and that he is confident, yes, well pleased rather to be absent from the body and to be present with You, Lord.

2 CORINTHIANS 5:7–8

24

INHERITANCE

Father God, grant my pastor the ability to see the magnitude of the inheritance that awaits him. Give him a vision of what You have in store for him even as I pray these Your words for him. In Jesus' name I pray. Amen.

God, in accordance with Your word . . .

I pray that whatever my pastor does, he will do it heartily, as to You, Lord, and not to men, knowing that from You he will receive the reward of the inheritance; for he serves the Lord Christ.

COLOSSIANS 3:23–24

———— † ————

I pray that my pastor has an inheritance incorruptible and undefiled and that does not fade away, reserved in heaven for him.

1 PETER 1:4

I pray that my pastor has been given
exceedingly great and precious promises,
that through these he may be a partaker of
the divine nature, having escaped the
corruption that is in the world through lust.

2 PETER 1:4

---------- † ----------

I commend my pastor to You, God, and to
the word of Your grace, which is able to
build him up and give him an inheritance
among all those who are sanctified.

ACTS 20:32

---------- † ----------

I pray that the Spirit Himself bears witness
with my pastor's spirit that he is a child of
Yours, and if a child, then an heir—an heir
of Yours and a joint heir with Christ, if indeed
he suffers with Him, that he may also be
glorified together with Him.

ROMANS 8:16–17

I pray that my pastor in You, Jesus, has obtained an inheritance, being predestined according to the purpose of Him who works all things according to the counsel of His will, that he who first trusted in You should be to the praise of His glory. In You, Jesus, he also trusted, after he heard the word of truth, the gospel of his salvation; in whom also, having believed, he was sealed with the Holy Spirit of promise, who is the guarantee of his inheritance until the redemption of the purchased possession, to the praise of His glory.

EPHESIANS 1:11–14

✟

I pray that my pastor always remembers that in Your house, God, are many mansions and if it were not so, Jesus would have told him. Help him to remember that Jesus has gone to prepare a place for him and if He goes and prepares a place for him, He will come again and receive him to Himself, that where He is, there he may be also.

JOHN 14:2–3

I pray Lord, that my pastor is aware that eye
has not seen, nor ear heard, nor have
entered into his heart the things which You
have prepared for those who love You.

1 CORINTHIANS 2:9

25

LONELY

Jesus, there are times in all of our lives when we feel lonely. My pastor surely experiences those same feelings at times in his life. Help him to sense the very power of Your word that I am praying today on his behalf. Use these prayers to remove lonely feelings from him. In Your name I pray. Amen.

God, in accordance with Your word . . .

I pray that my pastor's conduct will be without covetousness, and that he will be content with such things as he has. For You, God, said, "I will never leave you nor forsake you."

HEBREWS 13:5

--- † ---

I pray that my pastor remembers Jesus' promise to be with him always, even to the end of the age.

MATTHEW 28:20

I pray that my pastor will fear not, for You, God, are with him. That he be not dismayed, for You are his God. I pray that You will strengthen him and that You will help him, and that You will uphold him with Your righteous right hand.

ISAIAH 41:10

—————— † ——————

I pray that my pastor realizes that You, God, count the number of the stars and call them all by name. I pray that he remembers that great is his Lord, and mighty in power and that Your understanding is infinite.

PSALM 147:4–5

—————— † ——————

I pray that neither death nor life, nor angels nor principalities nor powers, nor things present nor things to come, nor height nor depth, nor any other created thing, shall be able to separate my pastor from Your love, God, which is in Christ Jesus his Lord.

ROMANS 8:38–39

I pray that my pastor remembers Your promise that You will not leave him as an orphan but that You will come to him.

JOHN 14:18

———— † ————

I pray that my pastor will be strong and of good courage and that he does not fear nor is he afraid, for You, the LORD his God, You are the One who goes with him. I pray that You will not leave him nor forsake him.

DEUTERONOMY 31:6

———— † ————

I pray that if my pastor's father and his mother forsake him, then You, LORD, will take care of him.

PSALM 27:10

———— † ————

I pray, O God, that You are my pastor's refuge and strength and a very present help in trouble.

PSALM 46:1

I pray that though the mountains shall depart and the hills be removed, Your kindness, God, shall not depart from my pastor, nor shall Your covenant of peace be removed from him.

ISAIAH 54:10

26

LOVE

Heavenly Father, You are love. Your words tell us of Your love for us. Today I ask that my prayers will find their way into my pastor's very being and that more than ever before he will sense Your love for him so that he can help us to better understand Your love for us. In Jesus' name I pray. Amen.

**God, in accordance
with Your word . . .**

I pray that my pastor will love others, for love is of You, God.

1 JOHN 4:7

———— † ————

I pray that my pastor understands the true meaning of love and that though he speaks with the tongues of men and of angels, but has not love, he has become sounding brass or a clanging cymbal. And though he has the gift of prophecy, and understands all mysteries and all knowledge, and though he has all faith, so that he could remove mountains, but has not love, he is nothing. And though he bestows all his goods to feed the poor, and though he gives his body to be burned, but has not love, it profits him nothing. I pray that he remembers that love suffers long and is kind; love does not envy; love does not parade itself, is not puffed up; does not behave rudely, does not seek its own, is not provoked, thinks no evil; does not rejoice in iniquity, but rejoices in the truth; bears all things, believes all things, hopes all things, endures all things. Help him to understand that love never fails. Help him to abide in faith, hope, love, these three; but the greatest of these is love.

1 CORINTHIANS 13:1–8, 13

---

†

I pray that my pastor loves Jesus and keeps His commandments. And my pastor who loves Jesus will be loved by You, God, and Jesus will love him and manifest Himself to him.

JOHN 14:21

I pray that my pastor understands that love
is not that he loved You, God, but that You
loved him and sent Your Son to be the
propitiation for his sins. And help him to
know that if You so loved him, he also ought
to love others.

1 JOHN 4:10–11

————— † —————

I pray that my pastor totally understands
that as You, God, loved Jesus, He also loves
him and he is to abide in His love.

JOHN 15:9

————— † —————

I pray, God, that You have loved my pastor
with an everlasting love and with
lovingkindness have drawn him to You.

JEREMIAH 31:3

————— † —————

I pray that You, God, love my pastor, because
he has loved Jesus, and has believed that
He came forth from You.

JOHN 16:27

I pray that You, God, will bring to my pastor's mind that it is Jesus' commandment that he love others as He has loved him.

JOHN 15:12

I pray that my pastor shall love You, the Lord his God, with all his heart, with all his soul, with all his mind, and with all his strength and that he shall love his neighbor as himself.

MARK 12:30–31

I pray that my pastor has known and believed the love that You, God, have for him and that he who loves You must love his brother also.

1 JOHN 4:16, 21

I pray that my pastor will realize that You, God, demonstrated Your own love toward him in that while he was still a sinner, Christ died for him.

ROMANS 5:8

I pray that You, God, so loved my pastor that You gave Your only begotten Son, that he who believes in Him should not perish but have everlasting life.

JOHN 3:16

———— † ————

I pray that neither death nor life, nor angels nor principalities nor powers, nor things present nor things to come, nor height nor depth, nor any other created thing, shall be able to separate my pastor from Your love, God, which is in Christ Jesus his Lord.

ROMANS 8:38–39

———— † ————

I pray that my pastor will take heed to the new commandment You gave to him that he love others as You have loved him, and that by this he will know that he is Your disciple, if he has love for others.

JOHN 13:34–35

27

MARITAL PROBLEMS

Lord God, I ask You to honor Your very words in this very sensitive area and to be with my pastor in every way possible as he deals with the problems in so many marriages. I love You and I love my pastor. Be with him now. In Jesus' name I ask You to bless the praying of Your word at all times. Thank You for hearing my prayers. Amen.

God, in accordance
with Your word . . .

I pray that as for my pastor and his house, they will serve You, LORD.

JOSHUA 24:15

---- † ----

I pray that my pastor has read that You, the LORD God, said, "It is not good that man should be alone; I will make him a helper comparable to him."

GENESIS 2:18

I pray that my pastor always understands
that a man shall leave his father and mother
and be joined to his wife, and they shall
become one flesh.

GENESIS 2:24

———— † ————

I pray that my pastor will teach others to
let all bitterness, wrath, anger, clamor, and
evil speaking be put away from them, with
all malice. And to be kind to one another,
tenderhearted, forgiving one another, just
as You, God, in Christ also forgave them.

EPHESIANS 4:31–32

———— † ————

I pray that my pastor will teach married
couples to be of one mind, having
compassion for one another, that they will
be tenderhearted and courteous, not
returning evil for evil or reviling for reviling,
but on the contrary blessing, knowing that
they were called to this, that they may inherit
a blessing.

1 PETER 3:8–9

I pray that my pastor will teach others to behave wisely in a perfect way and to walk within their house with a perfect heart.

PSALM 101:2

———— † ————

I pray that my pastor will teach married couples to trust in You, LORD, with all their hearts, and lean not on their own understanding and that in all their ways they acknowledge You, O God, and that You shall direct their paths.

PROVERBS 3:5–6

———— † ————

I pray that my pastor will teach married couples to purify their souls in obeying the truth through the Spirit in sincere love of each other, that they will love one another fervently with a pure heart.

1 PETER 1:22

I pray that my pastor remembers that hatred
stirs up strife, but love covers all sins.

PROVERBS 10:12

28
NEEDS

Lord, like everyone else, my pastor too has needs.
In many cases You and You alone know what those
needs are. I ask You now to meet those needs in his
life and to use him as a way to meet our needs.
Please honor Your words as I now pray them to You
on behalf of my pastor. I pray these prayers in
Jesus' name. Amen.

God, in accordance
with Your word . . .

I pray that my pastor will delight himself
also in You, LORD, and that You shall
give him the desires of his heart.

PSALM 37:4

— † —

I pray that You, God, will open Your hand
and satisfy the desire of my pastor.

PSALM 145:16

I pray that You, LORD, will guide my pastor continually.

ISAIAH 58:11

———— † ————

I pray that my pastor will not spend wages for what does not satisfy and that he will listen carefully to You, God, and will let his soul delight itself in abundance.

ISAIAH 55:2

———— † ————

I pray that whatever things my pastor asks for in prayer, believing, he will receive.

MATTHEW 21:22

———— † ————

I pray, Lord Jesus, that if my pastor abides in You and Your words abide in him, he will ask what he desires, and it shall be done for him.

JOHN 15:7

I pray, Jesus, that if my pastor asks anything
in Your name, You will do it.

JOHN 14:14

———— † ————

I pray that my pastor will ask in Your name,
Jesus, and he will receive, that his joy may
be full.

JOHN 16:24

———— † ————

I pray that my pastor shall know the truth,
and the truth shall make him free.

JOHN 8:32

———— † ————

I pray that You, the God and Father of our
Lord Jesus Christ, have blessed my pastor
with every spiritual blessing in the heavenly
places in Christ.

EPHESIANS 1:3

I pray that my pastor can do all things
through Christ who strengthens him.

PHILIPPIANS 4:13

———————— † ————————

I pray that You, my God, shall supply all my
pastor's needs according to Your riches in
glory by Christ Jesus.

PHILIPPIANS 4:19

———————— † ————————

I pray that if my pastor's heart does not
condemn him, he has confidence toward
You, God. And whatever he asks he
receives from You, because he keeps Your
commandments and does those things that
are pleasing in Your sight.

1 JOHN 3:21–22

29

OBEDIENCE

God, You have made it clear that obedience is more important to You than is sacrifice. I ask You to help my pastor be obedient to You in every way and in every situation. Having asked You for it in Jesus' name, I believe that it will happen and I thank You in His name. Amen.

God, in accordance with Your word . . .

I pray that my pastor recognizes the fact that You, God, have set before him today a blessing and a curse: the blessing, if he obeys the commandments of the LORD his God, which You have commanded him today; and the curse, if he does not obey the commandments of the LORD his God, but turns aside from the way which You command him today, to go after other gods which he has not known.

DEUTERONOMY 11:26–28

I pray that my pastor never forgets that to obey is better than sacrifice.

1 SAMUEL 15:22

———— † ————

I pray that my pastor will heed Your commandments, O God, so that his peace will be like a river, and his righteousness like the waves of the sea.

ISAIAH 48:18

———— † ————

I pray, O God, that my pastor will obey Your voice, and You will be his God, and he shall be Your child. And that he will walk in all the ways that You have commanded him, that it may be well with him.

JEREMIAH 7:23

———— † ————

I pray, Lord Jesus, that my pastor loves You and keeps Your commandments.

JOHN 14:15

I pray that my pastor knows that he ought
to obey You rather than men.

ACTS 5:29

———— † ————

I pray Jesus, that my pastor will always keep
Your commandments.

1 JOHN 2:3

———— † ————

I pray that my pastor will walk in Your
ways, God, to keep Your statutes and Your
commandments, and that You will lengthen
his days.

1 KINGS 3:14

———— † ————

I pray that You, God, will teach my pastor
to do Your will, for You are his God.

PSALM 143:10

I pray that my pastor will learn Your statutes,
O God, and be careful to observe them. I
pray that he will be careful to do as You,
the LORD his God, have commanded him and
that he shall not turn aside to the right hand
or to the left. I pray that he will walk in all
the ways which You have commanded him,
that he may live and that it may be well with
him, and that You may prolong his days.

DEUTERONOMY 5:1, 32–33

†

I pray that whatever my pastor does, he
does it heartily, as to the Lord and not
to men.

COLOSSIANS 3:23

30

PATIENCE

Lord Jesus, perhaps more than any other person, a pastor must have patience. He must wait on committees to act. He must wait on many of us to grow in Your word. I pray for my pastor what You have already declared in Your word, and I ask You to honor it in my pastor's life. Bless now the praying of Your word. Amen.

**God, in accordance
with Your word . . .**

I pray that whatever things were written
before were written for my pastor's learning,
that he through the patience and comfort
of the Scriptures might have hope. Now may
You, the God of patience and comfort, grant
my pastor to be like-minded toward others,
according to Christ Jesus.

ROMANS 15:4–5

I pray that my pastor will glory in
tribulations, knowing that tribulation
produces perseverance; and perseverance,
character; and character, hope.

ROMANS 5:3–4

———— † ————

I pray that my pastor will rest in You, LORD,
and that he will wait patiently for You. I pray
that he does not fret because of him who
prospers in his way or because of the man
who brings wicked schemes to pass. I pray
that he will cease from anger, and forsake
wrath and that he does not fret—it only
causes harm.

PSALM 37:7–8

———— † ————

I pray that my pastor will wait patiently for
You, LORD, and that You will incline Yourself
to him and hear his cry.

PSALM 40:1

I pray that my pastor will imitate those who through faith and patience inherit the promises.

HEBREWS 6:12

---------- † ----------

I pray that my pastor does not cast away his confidence, which has great reward. For he has need of endurance, so that after he has done Your will, God, he may receive his promise.

HEBREWS 10:35–36

---------- † ----------

I pray that my pastor will not hasten in his spirit to be angry, for anger rests in the bosom of fools.

ECCLESIASTES 7:9

---------- † ----------

I pray that the fruit of the Spirit in my pastor is love, joy, peace, longsuffering, kindness, goodness, faithfulness, gentleness, and self-control.

GALATIANS 5:22–23

I pray that since my pastor is surrounded
by so great a cloud of witnesses, let him lay
aside every weight, and the sin which so
easily ensnares him, and let him run with
endurance the race that is set before him.

HEBREWS 12:1

———— † ————

I pray that my pastor will wait on You, LORD,
and that he shall renew his strength. I pray
that he shall mount up with wings like eagles
and that he will run and not be weary and
walk and not faint.

ISAIAH 40:31

———— † ————

I pray that my pastor will hope and wait
quietly for Your salvation, O Lord.

LAMENTATIONS 3:26

———— † ————

I pray that my pastor will hope for what he
does not see and eagerly wait for it with
perseverance.

ROMANS 8:25

I pray that my pastor will wait on You, LORD, and that he will be of good courage. I also pray that You will strengthen his heart and that he will wait on You.

PSALM 27:14

———— † ————

I pray that my pastor understands that the testing of his faith produces patience and that he should let patience have its perfect work, that he may be perfect and complete, lacking nothing.

JAMES 1:3–4

———— † ————

I pray that my pastor will be patient until Your coming, Lord. I pray that he will see how the farmer waits for the precious fruit of the earth, waiting patiently for it until it receives the early and latter rain and that he will be patient, for Your coming is near.

JAMES 5:7–8

31

PEACE

Heavenly Father, I ask You today to give perfect peace to my pastor. It is Your words that I pray in Jesus' name, and I thank You for hearing and answering these my prayers. Amen.

God, in accordance
with Your word . . .

I pray that You will keep my pastor in
perfect peace, whose mind is stayed on You,
because he trusts in You.

ISAIAH 26:3

———————— † ————————

I pray that Your kindness, God, shall not
depart from my pastor, nor shall Your
covenant of peace be removed from him.

ISAIAH 54:10

I pray that my pastor will lie down in peace, and sleep; for You alone, O LORD, make him dwell in safety.

PSALM 4:8

———— † ————

I pray, O LORD, that You will give strength to my pastor and that You will bless him with peace.

PSALM 29:11

———— † ————

I pray that You, Jesus, have left peace with my pastor. I pray that his heart will not be troubled, neither will he be afraid.

JOHN 14:27

———— † ————

I pray that my pastor who has been justified by faith, will have peace with You, God, through his Lord Jesus Christ.

ROMANS 5:1

I pray that Jesus Himself is my pastor's peace.

EPHESIANS 2:14

———— † ————

I pray that my pastor will be anxious for
nothing, but in everything by prayer and
supplication, with thanksgiving, will let
his requests be made known to You, God;
and Your peace which surpasses all
understanding, will guard his heart and mind
through Christ Jesus.

PHILIPPIANS 4:6–7

———— † ————

I pray that the peace of God will rule in my
pastor's heart.

COLOSSIANS 3:15

Lord God, my pastor is in need of Your power. He needs Your power to do all that he does for Your work as he strives to teach us and to reach others for You. Honor the praying of Your word and more than ever before bring Your power into the life of my pastor. It is in the powerful name of Jesus that I offer up Your words to You in prayer for my pastor. Thank You for hearing and answering each of these prayers. Amen.

**God, in accordance
with Your word . . .**

I pray that my pastor will take pleasure in infirmities, in reproaches, in needs, in persecutions, in distresses, for Christ's sake. For when he is weak, then he is strong.

2 CORINTHIANS 12:10

I pray that in all things my pastor is more than a conqueror through Jesus who loved him.

ROMANS 8:37

———— † ————

I pray that my pastor can do all things through Christ who strengthens him.

PHILIPPIANS 4:13

———— † ————

I pray that whatever my pastor asks in Your name that You will do, that the Father may be glorified in the Son.

JOHN 14:13

———— † ————

I pray that You, God, are able to make all grace abound toward my pastor, that he, always having all sufficiency in all things, may have an abundance for every good work.

2 CORINTHIANS 9:8

I pray, Jesus, that Your grace is sufficient for my pastor, for Your strength is made perfect in weakness.

2 CORINTHIANS 12:9

— † —

I pray that my pastor will see the exceeding greatness of Your power, God, toward him who believes, according to the working of Your mighty power.

EPHESIANS 1:19

— † —

I pray, O God, that You are able to do exceedingly abundantly above all that my pastor asks or thinks, according to the power that works in him.

EPHESIANS 3:20

33

PRAISE

Heavenly Father, all of us were created to praise
You. I petition You today to put into my pastor's
heart a consistent desire to praise You at all times.
These words of Yours are my prayers for my pastor.
In Jesus' name I pray. Amen.

**God, in accordance
with Your word . . .**

I pray Lord God, that my pastor will sing
praises to You and that he will declare Your
deeds among the people.

PSALM 9:11

———— † ————

I pray that my pastor will sing to You, LORD,
as long as he lives.

PSALM 104:33

I pray that every day my pastor will bless
You, God, and will praise Your name forever
and ever.

PSALM 145:2

✝

I pray that my pastor will know that great
is the LORD, and greatly to be praised and
that Your greatness is unsearchable.

PSALM 145:3

✝

I pray that my pastor's tongue shall speak
of Your righteousness, Lord, and of Your
praise all the day long.

PSALM 35:28

✝

I pray, O Lord, that You will open my pastor's
lips and his mouth shall show forth Your
praise.

PSALM 51:15

I pray, O Lord, that my pastor will praise
You.

ISAIAH 12:1

———— † ————

I pray that my pastor will give You thanks,
O Lord God Almighty, the One who is and
who was and who is to come, because You
have taken Your great power and reigned.

REVELATION 11:17

———— † ————

I pray that my pastor will hope continually,
O God, and will praise You yet more and
more.

PSALM 71:14

———— † ————

I pray that my pastor will enter into Your
gates with thanksgiving, and into Your courts
with praise.

PSALM 100:4

I pray that You, Lord, are my pastor's strength and song, and that You have become his salvation; that You are his God, and that he will praise You.

EXODUS 15:2

———— † ————

I pray that my pastor will proclaim the name of the Lord and ascribe greatness to You his God.

DEUTERONOMY 32:3

———— † ————

I pray that my pastor will proclaim, "The Lord lives! Blessed be my Rock! Let God be exalted, the Rock of my salvation!"

2 SAMUEL 22:47

———— † ————

I pray that my pastor always remembers that You, Lord, are great and greatly to be praised.

1 CHRONICLES 16:25

I pray that my pastor will bless You, LORD, at all times and that Your praise shall continually be in his mouth.

PSALM 34:1

———— † ————

I pray that You have put a new song in my pastor's mouth—Praise to his God.

PSALM 40:3

———— † ————

I pray that my pastor realizes that great is the LORD, and greatly to be praised.

PSALM 48:1

———— † ————

I pray that my pastor prays, "Blessed be the Lord, who daily loads me with benefits."

PSALM 68:19

———— † ————

I pray that my pastor will praise You, LORD!

PSALM 146:1

I pray that my pastor will give thanks to You,
Lord, for You are good! For Your mercy
endures forever.

PSALM 106:1

†

I pray that You will let my pastor's soul live,
O God, and it shall praise You.

PSALM 119:175

†

I pray that my pastor will praise You, God,
for he is fearfully and wonderfully made.
Marvelous are Your works, and that his soul
knows very well.

PSALM 139:14

†

I pray that my pastor will continually offer
the sacrifice of praise to You, God, that is,
the fruit of his lips, giving thanks to Your
name.

HEBREWS 13:15

I pray that my pastor's mouth shall speak
the praise of You, God.

PSALM 145:21

———————— † ————————

I pray that my pastor will praise You, God,
for Your mighty acts and that he will praise
You according to Your excellent greatness!

PSALM 150:2

34

PROTECTION

Lord God, Satan would like nothing more than to destroy the ministry of my pastor. I pray Your very words today in order to put a hedge of Your protection around my pastor. The words I pray are Your words straight from Your Bible. Protect him at all times through the praying of Your word in Jesus' name. Amen.

God, in accordance
with Your word . . .

I pray that my pastor's LORD God, who goes before him, will fight for him.

DEUTERONOMY 1:30

———— † ————

I pray that if my pastor will indeed obey Your voice, God, and do all that You speak, then You will be an enemy to his enemies and an adversary to his adversaries.

EXODUS 23:22

I pray that no weapon formed against my
pastor shall prosper, and every tongue which
rises against him in judgment, You, God,
shall condemn.

ISAIAH 54:17

---------- † ----------

I pray that Jesus has given my pastor the
authority to trample on serpents and
scorpions, and over all the power of the
enemy, and nothing shall by any means hurt
him.

LUKE 10:19

---------- † ----------

I pray that You, Lord, are faithful, who will
establish my pastor and guard him from the
evil one.

2 THESSALONIANS 3:3

---------- † ----------

I pray that if God is for my pastor, who can
be against him?

ROMANS 8:31

35

REBELLIOUS

Lord God, I pray that my pastor will never be a rebellious person in any way. Through the praying of Your word, keep him free from any rebellious spirit or attitude. I pray to You and I thank You in Jesus' precious name. Amen.

**God, in accordance
with Your word . . .**

I pray that my pastor, by doing good, may put to silence the ignorance of foolish men.

1 PETER 2:15

---------- † ----------

I pray that if my pastor is willing and obedient he shall eat the good of the land.

ISAIAH 1:19

I pray that my pastor will gird up the loins of his mind, be sober, and rest his hope fully upon the grace that is to be brought to him at the revelation of Jesus Christ; as an obedient child, not conforming himself to the former lusts, as in his ignorance; but as You, God, who called him are Holy, he also is to be holy in all his conduct.

1 PETER 1:13–15

---------- † ----------

I pray that my pastor is aware that rebellion is as the sin of witchcraft.

1 SAMUEL 15:23

---------- † ----------

I pray that my pastor will be like Jesus and humble himself and become obedient.

PHILIPPIANS 2:8

---------- † ----------

I pray that like You, Jesus, my pastor learns obedience by the things he suffers.

HEBREWS 5:8

I pray that my pastor will obey those who rule over him, and be submissive, for they watch out for his soul, as those who must give account.

HEBREWS 13:17

———— † ————

I pray that my pastor knows that You resist the proud, but give grace to the humble and that he will humble himself under Your mighty hand, that You, God, may exalt him in due time.

1 PETER 5:5–6

———— † ————

I pray that my pastor will submit to You, God. That he will resist the devil and the devil will flee from him.

JAMES 4:7

———— † ————

I pray that while my pastor was once darkness, now he is light in the Lord and that he will walk as a child of light.

EPHESIANS 5:8

I pray that my pastor knows and understands that no grave trouble will overtake the righteous, but the wicked shall be filled with evil.

PROVERBS 12:21

———— † ————

I pray that my pastor will no longer walk in the futility of his mind.

EPHESIANS 4:17

———— † ————

I pray that my pastor does not let sin reign in his mortal body, that he should obey it in its lusts. I also pray that he does not present his members as instruments of unrighteousness to sin, but presents himself to You, God, as being alive from the dead, and his members as instruments of righteousness to God. For sin shall not have dominion over him, for he is not under law but under grace.

ROMANS 6:12–14

36

SALVATION

Lord, of all my pastor's responsibilities, the most important of all is to lead others to the salvation that You have prepared for those who accept Jesus as their Lord and Savior. Help him to preach, teach, and tell of Your wonderful free gift of salvation. Let it always be the most important thing in his life. In Jesus' name I pray Your words for my pastor. Amen.

God, in accordance with Your word . . .

I pray that my pastor will always teach that Jesus said, "He who believes in Me has everlasting life."

JOHN 6:47

———— † ————

I pray that my pastor remembers that Jesus has come to seek and to save that which was lost.

LUKE 19:10

I pray, Lord Jesus, that my pastor will come to understand what You meant when You said, "Therefore whoever confesses Me before men, him I will also confess before My Father who is in heaven."

MATTHEW 10:32

———— † ————

I pray that if my pastor will confess with his mouth the Lord Jesus and believe in his heart that God raised Him from the dead, he will be saved. For with his heart he believes unto righteousness, and with his mouth confession is made unto salvation.

ROMANS 10:9–10

———— † ————

I pray that it is not by works of righteousness which my pastor has done, but according to Your mercy You saved him, through the washing of regeneration and renewing of the Holy Spirit, whom You poured out on him abundantly through Jesus Christ his Savior.

TITUS 3:5–6

I pray that You, God, so loved my pastor
that You gave Your only begotten Son, that
if my pastor believes in Him he should not
perish but have everlasting life.

JOHN 3:16

———— † ————

I pray that You did not send Your Son into
the world to condemn my pastor, but that
my pastor through Him might be saved.

JOHN 3:17

———— † ————

I pray that this will be my pastor's testimony:
that You, God, have given him eternal life,
and this life is in Your Son.

1 JOHN 5:11

———— † ————

I pray that by grace my pastor has been
saved through faith, and that not of himself;
it is the gift of God, not of works, lest he
should boast.

EPHESIANS 2:8–9

I pray that You, God, have saved my pastor and called him with a holy calling, not according to his works, but according to Your own purpose and grace which was given to him in Christ Jesus before time began.

2 TIMOTHY 1:9

---

†

I pray that Jesus stands at the door and knocks and if my pastor hears His voice and opens the door, He will come in to him and dine with him, and him with Him.

REVELATION 3:20

---

†

I pray that my pastor has been born again, not of corruptible seed but incorruptible, through Your word which lives and abides forever.

1 PETER 1:23

37

SATAN DEFEATED

Heavenly Father, Satan is my pastor's enemy. He will do everything that he can do to destroy my pastor. I pray that every attack of Satan in my pastor's life will be defeated. Thank You, God, in the powerful name of Jesus. Amen.

God, in accordance with Your word . . .

I pray that my pastor will be strong in You, Lord, and in the power of Your might. I pray that he will put on the whole armor of God, that he may be able to stand against the wiles of the devil. For he does not wrestle against flesh and blood, but against principalities, against powers, against the rulers of the darkness of this age, against spiritual hosts of wickedness in the heavenly places. I pray that he will take up Your whole armor, God, that he may be able to withstand in the evil day, and having done all, to stand. I pray that he has girded his waist with truth, having put on the breastplate of righteousness, and having shod his feet with the preparation of the gospel of peace and above all, taking the shield of faith with which he will be able to quench all the fiery darts of the wicked one. I pray that he also takes the helmet of salvation, and the sword of the Spirit, which is the word of God; praying always with all prayer and supplication in the Spirit, being watchful to this end with all perseverance and supplication for all the saints.

EPHESIANS 6:10–18

———— † ————

I pray that You, God, will open my pastor's eyes, in order to turn them from darkness to light, and from the power of Satan to You, that he may receive forgiveness of sins and an inheritance among those who are sanctified by faith in Jesus.

ACTS 26:18

I pray that You preserve the soul of my
pastor and deliver him out of the hand of
the wicked.

PSALM 97:10

———————— † ————————

I pray for my pastor that the Son of God
was manifested that He might destroy the
works of the devil.

1 JOHN 3:8

———————— † ————————

I pray for my pastor that he puts off,
concerning his former conduct, the old
man which grows corrupt according to the
deceitful lusts and be renewed in the spirit
of his mind and that he put on the new man
which was created according to You, God,
in true righteousness and holiness.

EPHESIANS 4:22–24

———————— † ————————

I pray that my pastor will not give place to
the devil.

EPHESIANS 4:27

I pray, Jesus, that my pastor knows that You
have disarmed principalities and powers,
and have made a public spectacle of them,
triumphing over them in it.

COLOSSIANS 2:15

---------- † ----------

I pray that my pastor understands that even
the angels who did not keep their proper
domain, but left their own abode, You have
reserved in everlasting chains under
darkness for the judgment of the great day.

JUDE 1:6

---------- † ----------

I pray that my pastor is strong and that the
word of God abides in him, and he has
overcome the wicked one.

1 JOHN 2:14

---------- † ----------

I do not pray, God, that You should take my
pastor out of the world, but that You should
keep him from the evil one.

JOHN 17:15

I pray that my pastor will be sober and vigilant, because his adversary the devil walks about like a roaring lion, seeking whom he may devour. I pray that he will resist him, steadfast in the faith, knowing that the same sufferings are experienced by other Christians in the world.

1 PETER 5:8–9

———— † ————

I pray that at this time my pastor will remember that Jesus went about doing good and healing all who were oppressed by the devil, for God was with Him.

ACTS 10:38

———— † ————

I pray that You, God, have delivered my pastor from the power of darkness and conveyed him into the kingdom of Jesus, in whom he has redemption through His blood, the forgiveness of sins.

COLOSSIANS 1:13–14

I pray that my pastor will submit to You,
God, and that he will resist the devil and
the devil will flee from him.

JAMES 4:7

———— † ————

I pray that neither death nor life, nor angels
nor principalities nor powers, nor things
present nor things to come, nor height nor
depth, nor any other created thing, shall be
able to separate my pastor from the love
of God which is in Christ Jesus his Lord.

ROMANS 8:38–39

———— † ————

I pray that while my pastor is hard pressed
on every side, yet not crushed; he is
perplexed, but not in despair; persecuted,
but not forsaken; struck down, but not
destroyed—always carrying about in his
body the dying of the Lord Jesus, that the
life of Jesus also may be manifested in his
body.

2 CORINTHIANS 4:8–10

I pray that in all things my pastor is more than a conqueror through Him who loved him.

ROMANS 8:37

---

†

I pray that the accuser of my pastor, who accuses him before God day and night, has been cast down. I pray that he overcame him by the blood of the Lamb and by the word of his testimony.

REVELATION 12:10–11

---

†

I pray that though my pastor walks in the flesh, he does not war according to the flesh. For the weapons of his warfare are not carnal but mighty in God for pulling down strongholds, casting down arguments and every high thing that exalts itself against the knowledge of God, bringing every thought into captivity to the obedience of Christ.

2 CORINTHIANS 10:3–5

I pray that my pastor has his senses exercised
to discern both good and evil.

HEBREWS 5:14

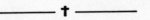

I pray, Lord, that You will guard my pastor
from the evil one.

2 THESSALONIANS 3:3

I pray that Your presence will go with my
pastor forever.

EXODUS 33:14

I pray that my pastor will have the mind of
Christ.

1 CORINTHIANS 2:16

I pray that my pastor will be strong and of
good courage; that he is not afraid, nor
dismayed, for You, the LORD his God, are
with him wherever he goes.

JOSHUA 1:9

I pray that You will preserve the soul of my pastor and that You will deliver him out of the hand of the wicked.

PSALM 97:10

———— † ————

I pray that You are my pastor's refuge, and that You will thrust out the enemy from before him.

DEUTERONOMY 33:27

———— † ————

I pray that the angel of the LORD encamps around my pastor who fears You and delivers him.

PSALM 34:7

———— † ————

I pray that my pastor will gird up the loins of his mind and be sober, and rest his hopes fully upon the grace that is to be brought to him at the revelation of Jesus Christ; as an obedient child, not conforming himself to the former lusts, as in his ignorance; but as You, God, who called him are holy, may he also be holy in all his conduct.

1 PETER 1:13–15

———— † ————

I pray that Satan will not take advantage of my pastor for he is not ignorant of his devices.

2 CORINTHIANS 2:11

———— † ————

I pray that my pastor knows that he does not live by bread alone, but by every word that proceeds from the mouth of God.

MATTHEW 4:4

———— † ————

I pray that my pastor will drive Satan away by worshiping the Lord his God, and Him only he shall serve.

MATTHEW 4:10

38

SECURITY

Lord, I know and understand that real security comes only from You. Today I pray Your security for my pastor. Through the praying of Your word give him the security that only You can give. In Jesus' name. Amen.

**God, in accordance
with Your word . . .**

I pray that my pastor is persuaded that neither death nor life, nor angels nor principalities nor powers, nor things present nor things to come, nor height nor depth, nor any other created thing, shall be able to separate him from the love of God which is in Christ Jesus his Lord.

ROMANS 8:38–39

I pray that in Jesus my pastor also trusted, after he heard the word of truth, the gospel of his salvation, in whom also, having believed, he was sealed with the Holy Spirit of promise.

EPHESIANS 1:13

———— † ————

I pray that surely goodness and mercy shall follow my pastor all the days of his life, and that he will dwell in the house of the LORD forever.

PSALM 23:6

———— † ————

I pray that my pastor is one of those who has come to You, Jesus, and who You will by no means cast out.

JOHN 6:37

———— † ————

I pray that my pastor does not grieve the Holy Spirit of God, by whom he was sealed for the day of redemption.

EPHESIANS 4:30

I pray that my pastor has heard Your voice
and that You know him, and that he follows
You and that You will give him eternal life,
and he shall never perish.

JOHN 10:27–28

———— † ————

I pray that You, God, who have begun a
good work in my pastor will complete it until
the day of Jesus Christ.

PHILIPPIANS 1:6

———— † ————

I pray, Lord, that Your faithfulness will
establish my pastor and guard him from the
evil one.

2 THESSALONIANS 3:3

———— † ————

I pray that You, God, are able to keep my
pastor from stumbling, and to present him
faultless before the presence of Your glory
with exceeding joy.

JUDE 1:24

39

SERVING GOD

Lord God, my pastor is one of Your chosen servants. He has been called to serve You. Help him, through the praying of Your word, to serve You as never before. Give him strength and wisdom and the desire to render to You the highest possible service that he can give. Direct him that he may serve You better than ever before. Thank You in Jesus' name. Amen.

**God, in accordance
with Your word . . .**

I pray that my pastor will walk after You, the LORD his God, and fear You, and keep Your commandments and obey Your voice, and that he shall serve You and hold fast to You.

DEUTERONOMY 13:4

I pray that my pastor knows that he cannot serve two masters; for either he will hate the one and love the other, or else he will be loyal to the one and despise the other. He cannot serve You and mammon.

MATTHEW 6:24

---------- † ----------

I pray that my pastor will serve You, the Lord his God, and You only he shall serve.

MATTHEW 4:10

---------- † ----------

I pray to You, God, that my pastor will present his body a living sacrifice, holy, acceptable to You, which is his reasonable service. I pray also that he will not be conformed to this world, but be transformed by the renewing of his mind, that he may prove what is that good and acceptable and perfect will of Yours.

ROMANS 12:1–2

I pray that my pastor will love You, the LORD his God, and walk in all Your ways, keeping Your commandments, and holding fast to You, and serving You with all his heart and with all his soul.

JOSHUA 22:5

————— † —————

I pray that my pastor will be kindly affectionate to others with brotherly love, in honor giving preference to others; not lagging in diligence, fervent in spirit, serving You, Lord; rejoicing in hope, patient in tribulation, continuing steadfastly in prayer; distributing to the needs of the saints, given to hospitality.

ROMANS 12:10–13

————— † —————

I pray that my pastor will fear You, the LORD his God, and walk in all Your ways and love You, and serve You, the LORD his God, with all his heart and with all his soul, and that

he will keep Your commandments and Your
statutes which You command him today for
his good.

DEUTERONOMY 10:12–13

———————— † ————————

I pray that my pastor does not turn aside
from following You, Lord, but serves You
with all his heart. I pray that he does not
turn aside, for then he would go after empty
things which cannot profit or deliver, for they
are nothing. For You will not forsake him,
for Your great name's sake, because it has
pleased You to make him Yours.

1 SAMUEL 12:20–22

———————— † ————————

I pray that my pastor will know You, God,
and serve You with a loyal heart and with
a willing mind; for You search all hearts and
understand all the intent of the thoughts. If
he seeks You, You will be found by him; but
if he forsakes You, You will cast him off
forever.

1 CHRONICLES 28:9

I pray, O God, that my pastor shall serve
You, the LORD his God.

EXODUS 23:25

———————— † ————————

I pray that my pastor has been delivered
from the law, having died to what he was
held by, so that he serves in the newness of
the Spirit and not in the oldness of the letter.

ROMANS 7:6

———————— † ————————

I pray that my pastor serves You, LORD, with
gladness and that he will come before Your
presence with singing. I pray that he will
know that You, Lord, are God and that it
is You who have made him, and not he
himself.

PSALM 100:2–3

40

SICKNESS

Heavenly Father, I pray that You will heal my pastor of any affliction that may come upon him and that You will restore his health to him. It is in the powerful name of Jesus that I pray these prayers to You. Amen.

God, in accordance with Your word . . .

I pray that You will heal my pastor, O Lord, and he shall be healed. Save him, and he shall be saved.

JEREMIAH 17:14

———— † ————

I pray that You will restore health to my pastor and heal his wounds.

JEREMIAH 30:17

I pray that my pastor will diligently heed Your voice, LORD God, and do what is right in Your sight and give ear to Your commandments and keep all Your statutes and that You will put no diseases on him.

EXODUS 15:26

---

†

I pray, O God, that Jesus was wounded for my pastor's transgressions and was bruised for his iniquities and by His stripes my pastor is healed.

ISAIAH 53:5

---

†

I pray that You heal all my pastor's diseases, and redeem his life from destruction.

PSALM 103:3–4

---

†

I pray that my pastor may prosper in all things and be in health just as his soul prospers.

3 JOHN 1:2

I pray that Jesus Himself bore my pastor's sins in His own body on the tree, and that my pastor, having died to sin, might live for righteousness—by whose stripes he was healed.

1 PETER 2:24

———— † ————

I pray, O God, that my pastor remembers that Jesus healed every sickness and every disease among the people.

MATTHEW 9:35

———— † ————

I pray that power goes out from You and heals my pastor.

LUKE 6:19

———— † ————

I pray that You have sent Your word and healed my pastor and delivered him from destruction.

PSALM 107:20

I pray that I am not worthy that You should come under my roof. But only speak a word, and my pastor will be healed.

MATTHEW 8:8

———— † ————

I pray that the prayer of faith will save my pastor from his sickness and that You, Lord, will raise him up. And if he has committed sins, he will be forgiven.

JAMES 5:15

41

SPIRITUAL GROWTH

Lord Jesus, none of us will ever know all that there is to know about You. I pray that my pastor, in addition to teaching us, will also study Your word for his continued spiritual growth and will endeavor to keep himself in accordance with Your word. Thank You for honoring Your words that I pray to You now. Amen.

**God, in accordance
with Your word . . .**

I pray that my pastor will beware, lest there be in him an evil heart of unbelief in departing from the living God. I pray that we will exhort him daily, while it is called "Today," lest he be hardened through the deceitfulness of sin.

HEBREWS 3:12–13

I pray that my pastor does not forget You, the LORD his God, by not keeping Your commandments, Your judgments, and Your statutes which You command him today. I pray that he shall remember the LORD his God, for it is You who gives him the power to get wealth.

DEUTERONOMY 8:11, 18

———— † ————

I pray that my pastor has not forgotten the name of his God, or stretched out his hands to a foreign god. Would You, God, not search this out? For You know the secrets of the heart.

PSALM 44:20–21

———— † ————

I pray that my pastor will be watchful, and strengthen the things which remain, that are ready to die, for he has not found his works perfect before You.

REVELATION 3:2

I pray that my pastor will take heed to himself, and diligently keep himself, lest he forget the things his eyes have seen, and lest they depart from his heart all the days of his life.

DEUTERONOMY 4:9

———— † ————

I pray that my pastor will look diligently lest he fall short of Your grace, God, and lest any root of bitterness spring up causing trouble, and by this he becomes defiled.

HEBREWS 12:15

———— † ————

I pray that after my pastor has escaped the pollution of the world through the knowledge of his Lord and Savior Jesus Christ, that he not become entangled in them and overcome.

2 PETER 2:20

42

STRENGTH

God, my pastor needs more strength than ever before. I pray Your word that You will increase his strength according to Your word. Help him to sense even now the filling of Your strength in his life. In Jesus' precious name I pray. Amen.

God, in accordance with Your word . . .

I pray that You give power to my pastor, who is weak, and that You increase his strength.

ISAIAH 40:29

———— † ————

I pray that my pastor shall wait on You, LORD, and that he shall renew his strength. I pray that he shall mount up with wings like eagles, that he shall run and not be weary, and that he shall walk and not faint.

ISAIAH 40:31

I pray that my pastor will fear not, for You are with him. I pray that he will not be dismayed, for You are his God. I pray that You will strengthen him and help him and that You will uphold him with Your righteous right hand.

ISAIAH 41:10

--- ✝ ---

I pray that You, LORD, are my pastor's rock and his fortress and his deliverer; his God, his strength, in whom he will trust; his shield and the horn of his salvation, his stronghold. I pray that he will call upon You, Lord, who are worthy to be praised; so shall he be saved from his enemies.

PSALM 18:2-3

--- ✝ ---

I pray that my pastor will be strengthened with all might, according to Your glorious power, God.

COLOSSIANS 1:11

I pray that You, LORD, are my pastor's light
and his salvation. Whom shall he fear?

PSALM 27:1

————— † —————

I pray that You will strengthen my pastor
according to Your word.

PSALM 119:28

————— † —————

I pray that my pastor can do all things
through Christ who strengthens him.

PHILIPPIANS 4:13

————— † —————

I pray that You, God, will grant my pastor,
according to the riches of Your glory, to be
strengthened with might through Your Spirit.

EPHESIANS 3:16

————— † —————

I pray that my pastor will be strong in You,
Lord, and in the power of Your might. I pray
that he will put on the whole armor of God,

that he may be able to stand against the wiles of the devil. For he does not wrestle against flesh and blood, but against principalities, against powers, against the rulers of the darkness of this age, against spiritual hosts of wickedness in the heavenly places.

EPHESIANS 6:10–12

———— † ————

I pray that my pastor will put on Your whole armor, God, that he may be able to withstand in the evil day, and having done all, to stand. I pray that he will stand therefore, having girded his waist with truth, having put on the breastplate of righteousness, and having shod his feet with the preparation of the gospel of peace; above all, taking the shield of faith with which he will be able to quench all the fiery darts of the wicked one. I pray also that he will take the helmet of salvation, and the sword of the Spirit, which is the word of God, praying always with all prayer and supplication in the Spirit.

EPHESIANS 6:13–18

43

TEMPTED

Jesus, my pastor is no different from anyone else when it comes to temptation. Satan will do everything in his power to tempt my pastor to do wrong. Today I pray to You to deliver my pastor out of temptations. I pray Your word for him in this area, and I trust You to do as Your word promises. In Your name I pray. Amen.

God, in accordance
with Your word ...

I pray that You, Lord, know how to deliver my pastor out of temptations.

2 PETER 2:9

———— † ————

I pray that sin shall not have dominion over my pastor, for he is not under law but under grace.

ROMANS 6:14

I pray, Lord, that Your word my pastor has hidden in his heart, that he might not sin against You.

PSALM 119:11

———— † ————

I pray that if my pastor confesses and forsakes his sins he will have mercy.

PROVERBS 28:13

———— † ————

I pray that if my pastor confesses his sins, You are faithful and just to forgive his sins and to cleanse him from all unrighteousness.

1 JOHN 1:9

———— † ————

I pray that no temptation has overtaken my pastor except such as is common to man; but You, God, are faithful, and will not allow him to be tempted beyond what he is able, but with the temptation You will also make the way of escape, that he may be able to bear it.

1 CORINTHIANS 10:13

I pray, Lord, that my pastor will not say when
he is tempted, "I am tempted by God"; for
You cannot be tempted by evil, nor do You
Yourself tempt anyone. For he is tempted
when he is drawn away by his own desires
and enticed. Then, when desire has
conceived, it gives birth to sin; and sin, when
it is full-grown, brings forth death. I pray that
my pastor will not be deceived.

JAMES 1:13–16

———————— † ————————

I pray that my pastor does not have a High
Priest who cannot sympathize with his
weaknesses, but was in all points tempted
as he is, yet without sin. Let him therefore
come boldly to the throne of grace, that he
may obtain mercy and find grace to help
in time of need.

HEBREWS 4:15–16

———————— † ————————

I pray, Jesus, that You are able to aid my
pastor who is tempted.

HEBREWS 2:18

I pray that my pastor will be sober and vigilant; because his adversary the devil walks about like a roaring lion, seeking whom he may devour. I pray that he will resist him, steadfast in the faith, knowing that the same sufferings are experienced by his Christian brothers in the world.

1 PETER 5:8–9

— † —

I pray that my pastor will be strong in You, Lord, and in Your might. I pray that he will put on Your whole armor, that he may be able to stand against the wiles of the devil and that above all, he takes the shield of faith with which he will be able to quench all the fiery darts of the wicked one.

EPHESIANS 6:10–11, 16

— † —

I pray that You, God, are able to keep my pastor from stumbling and to present him faultless before the presence of Your glory with exceeding joy.

JUDE 1:24

I pray that He who is in my pastor, is greater than he who is in the world.

1 JOHN 4:4

———— † ————

I pray, Lord, that my pastor will count it all joy when he falls into various trials, knowing that the testing of his faith produces patience. I pray that blessed is my pastor who endures temptation; for when he has been approved, he will receive the crown of life which You have promised to those who love You.

JAMES 1:2–3, 12

———— † ————

I pray that my pastor will resist the devil and that the devil will flee from him.

JAMES 4:7

———— † ————

I pray that in this my pastor will greatly rejoice, though now for a little while, if need be, he has been grieved by various trials,

that the genuineness of his faith, being much
more precious than gold that perishes,
though it is tested by fire, may be found to
praise, honor, and glory at the revelation
of Jesus Christ.

1 PETER 1:6–7

44

TROUBLES

Lord, I ask You today to keep troubles away from my pastor. Your word says that You will allow no more troubles than he can bear. I pray Your word over my pastor in order for him to overcome any troubles that he may have. Please honor Your words in my prayers and take care of and strengthen him. It is in the authority of the name of Jesus that I pray. Amen.

God, in accordance with Your word . . .

I pray that my pastor will be anxious for nothing, but in everything by prayer and supplication, with thanksgiving, will let his requests be made known to You, God, and Your peace, which surpasses all understanding, will guard his heart and mind through Christ Jesus.

PHILIPPIANS 4:6–7

I pray that my pastor shall obtain joy and gladness and that sorrow and sighing shall flee away.

ISAIAH 51:11

———————— † ————————

I pray that You will comfort my pastor in all his tribulation, that he may be able to comfort those who are in any trouble, with the comfort with which he himself is comforted by You.

2 CORINTHIANS 1:4

———————— † ————————

I pray that my pastor does not worry about tomorrow, for tomorrow will worry about its own things.

MATTHEW 6:34

———————— † ————————

I pray that all things work together for good to my pastor who loves You, God, to him who is called according to Your purpose.

ROMANS 8:28

I pray that my pastor will be glad and rejoice in Your mercy, God, for You have considered his trouble. You have known his soul in adversities, and have not shut him up into the hand of the enemy. You have set his feet in a wide place.

PSALM 31:7–8

✝

I pray that my pastor's help comes from You, LORD, who made heaven and earth.

PSALM 121:2

✝

I pray that my pastor will come boldly to the throne of grace, that he may obtain mercy and find grace to help him in time of need.

HEBREWS 4:16

✝

I pray that my pastor will cast all his cares upon You, for You care for him.

1 PETER 5:7

I pray, O God, that my pastor always
remembers that You are good, a stronghold
in his day of trouble; and that You know that
he trusts in You.

NAHUM 1:7

―――――― † ――――――

I pray that though my pastor is hard pressed
on every side, he is not crushed; he is
perplexed, but not in despair; persecuted,
but not forsaken; struck down, but not
destroyed.

2 CORINTHIANS 4:8

―――――― † ――――――

I pray, God, that when my pastor passes
through the waters, You will be with him.
And through the rivers, they shall not
overflow him. When he walks through the
fire, he shall not be burned, nor shall the
flame scorch him. For You are the Lord his
God.

ISAIAH 43:2–3

I pray that my pastor will not let his heart be troubled. I pray that he believes in You, God, and also in Jesus.

JOHN 14:1

———— † ————

I pray that though my pastor walks in the midst of trouble, You, God, will revive him. You will stretch out Your hand against the wrath of his enemies, and Your right hand will save him.

PSALM 138:7

45

WAITING ON GOD

Heavenly Father, my prayers today will be Your very words. Hear my prayers and help my pastor to wait on You. And help him to teach us to do the same. I pray everything in Jesus' wonderful name. Amen.

God, in accordance
with Your word . . .

I pray that my pastor will say in that day: "Behold, this is my God. I have waited for Him, and He will save me. This is the LORD; I have waited for Him. I will be glad and rejoice in His salvation."

ISAIAH 25:9

———————— † ————————

I pray that my pastor has become a partaker of Christ if he holds the beginning of his confidence steadfast to the end.

HEBREWS 3:14

I pray that my pastor waits for You, LORD, that his soul waits, and in Your word he does hope.

PSALM 130:5

———— † ————

I pray that my pastor will wait on You, LORD, and that he will be of good courage. I pray also that You will strengthen his heart.

PSALM 27:14

———— † ————

I pray that my pastor's soul waits silently for You alone, and that his expectation is from You.

PSALM 62:5

———— † ————

I pray, O God, that my pastor will hold fast the confession of his hope without wavering, for You who promised are faithful.

HEBREWS 10:23

I pray that my pastor shall wait on You, LORD, and that he shall renew his strength. I pray also that he shall mount up with wings like eagles and that he shall run and not be weary and walk and not faint.

ISAIAH 40:31

———— † ————

I pray that my pastor's soul waits for You, LORD, that You are his help and his shield.

PSALM 33:20

46

WORRIED

Heavenly Father, today I pray Your word over the worries of my pastor. You have promised to not let his heart be troubled if he will cast his cares on You. I pray that all worry will flee from him and that his joy will return to him. I pray in Jesus' name. Amen.

God, in accordance with Your word . . .

I pray that my pastor will let not his heart be troubled.

JOHN 14:1

———— † ————

I pray that my pastor will cast all his cares upon You, God, for You care for him.

1 PETER 5:7

I pray that my pastor will lie down in peace,
and sleep; for You alone, O LORD, make him
dwell in safety.

PSALM 4:8

———— † ————

I pray that You, God, will keep my pastor
in perfect peace, he whose mind is stayed
on You, because he trusts in You.

ISAIAH 26:3

———— † ————

I pray that my pastor will let Your peace rule
in his heart.

COLOSSIANS 3:15

———— † ————

I pray that my pastor will be anxious for
nothing, but in everything by prayer and
supplication, with thanksgiving, will let his
requests be made known to You, God, and
Your peace, which surpasses all
understanding, will guard his heart and mind
through Christ Jesus.

PHILIPPIANS 4:6–7

I pray that You shall supply all my pastor's needs according to Your riches in glory by Christ Jesus.

PHILIPPIANS 4:19

———— † ————

I pray that my pastor will not worry about his life, what he will eat or what he will drink; nor about his body, what he will put on. I pray that he will seek first the kingdom of God and Your righteousness, and all these things shall be added to him.

MATTHEW 6:25, 33

———— † ————

I pray, Lord, that when my pastor lies down, he will not be afraid. I pray that he will lie down and his sleep will be sweet.

PROVERBS 3:24

———— † ————

I pray that my pastor will say of You, LORD, "He is my refuge and my fortress; my God, in Him I will trust."

PSALM 91:2

I pray, O God, that great peace has my pastor who loves Your law, and nothing can cause him to stumble.

PSALM 119:165

———————— † ————————

I pray, Jesus, that Your peace You leave with my pastor and that Your peace You give to him; not as the world gives do You give to him. Let not his heart be troubled, neither let it be afraid.

JOHN 14:27

Seminars conducted by Lee Roberts include *Praying God's Will*, *Avoiding Failure in Your Christian Walk*, and *The Businessman, the Salesman, and God!*

More information on these seminars can be obtained by writing Lee Roberts, P.O. Box 671465, Marietta, GA 30067-0025, or by calling 404-956-8550.